Mastering the Skills of

LIVE

PRESENTATIONS

Giving You the Skills to Achieve Success

Matthew H. Herynk, Ph.D.

Publication Date: 2011

Matthew H Herynk, Ph.D

Copyright 2010
Publishing division of ProAbstract LLC
Topeka, KS

Mastering the Skills of Live Presentations

ISBN 9781453861141

Cover Photograph by Rachel Lock

About the Cover

Acorns

The acorn, as with any seed, contains everything it needs to continue creating more things after its own kind.

Yet, an acorn has to fall on fertile soil before it will take root and grow. The conditions have to be just right. The ground has to be properly prepared and fertilized to be ready to receive it.

But once it settles, the roots grow deep and strong. I noticed when we were trying to take some pictures of the seedlings, I couldn't pull them out of the ground because they were already so firmly rooted.

The acorn just is. It doesn't think about what it is going to be or wish to be something else. It just exists and becomes what it was always destined to be.

—Rachel Lock, Photographer

Nurturing a Seed

We are all too familiar with the metaphor of the tiniest acorn growing into the mighty oak tree. The acorn has been chosen for the cover art because it represents the beginning of a process resulting in the mighty oak. While finding acorns to photograph we noticed that the vast majority of acorns were eaten, crushed, or simply rotted away. Only a small fraction of this powerful metaphor falls in the right place, gets enough water and nurturing, to produce a seedling, and an even smaller fraction of these seedlings receive enough nurturing to grow into a mighty oak. With proper nurturing and care, you can acquire the skills to become a great speaker.

—Matthew H Herynk, Author

Acknowledgments

This book is dedicated to my friends and family for all of their support and advice during the writing process. Especially my parents Jim and Diane, and my children Emma and Luke.

To all the mentors I have had along the way, Gerald, Bob, Gary, Lee, Janet, Josh, Suzanne, John, and Lee. Thank you for patiently and honestly providing feedback and listening to my presentations over and over again.

Special thanks to Wendy Ash Long for her hours of editing and Rachel Lock for the cover photograph.

Contents

Preface

This book has been written with the novice or beginner speaker in mind. However, if you are an accomplished speaker, you will undoubtedly come away with a few tidbits and morsels that will make you a better speaker. Covered in this book are the basics of how to get through a live presentation with confidence and credibility. If you feel that you have already developed the skills discussed in this book, and you are looking to increase your skills to the next level and become a dynamic speaker, I suggest that you read entire books devoted to one particular skill and practice, practice, practice. Also, study the people who have the skills you wish to acquire. If you are just beginning your speaking career, or if you only plan on giving a few live presentations each year, this book is for you. Follow the advice, exercises, and challenges given and you will be on your way to mastering the art of live presentations.

At the end of each chapter you will find exercises and challenges; however, not all chapters have both. The exercises should be easy to do, and they will help you practice skills that will make you a more effective speaker. The challenges are more difficult and are designed to make you observe your own behaviors or step out of your comfort zone. These are real keys to improving your presentation skills—*don't miss them!*

That circumstances grow out of thought every man knows who has for any length of time practiced self-control and self-purification, for he will have noticed that the alteration in his circumstances has been in exact ration with his altered mental condition. So true is this that when a man earnestly applies himself to remedy the defects in his character, and makes swift and marked progress, he passes rapidly through a succession of vicissitudes.

—James Allen, <u>As a Man Thinketh</u>

Section I

Basic Skills

A strong foundation is imperative to building a great and lasting edifice.

Chapter 1

Talk to Someone New Every Day

Small talk is the icebreaker that clears the way for more intimate conversation, laying the foundation for a stronger relationship. People who excel at small talk are experts at making others feel included, valued, and comfortable.

—Debra Fine, <u>The Fine Art of Small Talk</u>

Public speaking usually involves talking to people you haven't met. After all, if they knew you well and wanted to hear what you had to say, they would call you on the phone or buy you lunch. Learning the art of small talk will go a long way to building confidence in public speaking. We have all met people who can walk into a room and hold a conversation with anyone about anything. They appear to be fearless in the face of new people; in fact, they may thrive on it. Of course, good sales people instantly come to mind— they have mastered the art of small talk.

"I want to give a seminar to a large group, why do I need to make small talk with people?" The answer isn't obvious from the outset, but mastering this skill will bring new friends, contacts, and opportunities to your life. If you have been asked (or told by your boss) to give a presentation, you will need to speak with many people to set up the details of the presentation, including the room, time limits, scope, etc. Each one of these people you will work with can help or hurt you, depending on how much they like you. If you can make small talk and identify with the secretary, he or she is more likely to help you, for example, by making sure everything is working properly and may even be able to provide valuable information, such as watch out for Mr. X. Alternatively, he may decide to take his coffee break when you arrive. You will undoubtedly meet with many old and new peers and colleagues—possibly even your next boss—when you are giving the talk. If formal meetings have not been set up, people will definitely come up before and after your talk to greet you, ask questions, and generally get to know you a little better. You can't hide from them.

The skill of making small talk allows you to speak with anyone, anywhere, anytime in a relaxed manner. Think of the confidence you will have if you know you can engage the person next to you at the grocery store, elevator, or any room you walk into. These skills will also come in handy as you read your audience during Q&A sessions (discussed in later chapters).

You may be asking, *"How will making small talk come in handy when someone asks a directed question?"* Small talk requires engaging another person by asking directed questions, paying attention, and listening. You must think on your feet to succinctly answer a question in order to connect with the person asking it.

Your personal network is dependent upon who you know and what they think of you. If you are held in high regard, you are likely to benefit from new people in your network. Since we all know that most jobs and opportunities arise from people in our network, being highly regarded in a large network is beneficial. The average person has almost 500 people in his or her network (McCormick, 2008). Therefore, if the 500 people in my network each have 500 people in their networks. That equals 250,000 people I can influence! **When you meet and connect with one new person, you enlarge your network by 500 people!** Think of the possibilities if we could leverage our entire network! You never know which one of those 250,000 people may want to hire you, make a big donation to your cause, or connect you with another important element of your personal goals.

Public speaking is an opportunity for you to be in the spotlight and to be in charge of the stage—

Make the most of it!

How to Make Small Talk with Anyone

There are many books, Web pages, blogs, and videos dedicated to helping people learn the art of small talk. I am a natural introvert, a nerdy scientist; I have a fear of new people, etc. Because of these naturally introverted traits, I have read many resources on making small talk, and yes, flirting. One common theme arises in all of these resources, whether you are using small talk to pass the time, fit in at a meeting, or trying to get a discount: *Pay attention to the other person.*

If the simple question, *"Hot enough for ya?"* elicits the response, *"Sure is, I had to wait until the sun went down to take my dog for a walk,"* you now know several things about the person that can be used to open up a conversation: 1) They have a dog. Ask about the dog, *"What kind of dog do you have? Do you have other pets? What are your favorite dog parks?"* etc. 2) They go for daily walks. You might ask, *"Where do you walk? How far do you go? What time do you like to go?"*

The key is to pay attention and to formulate a follow-up question that is based on the answer given. If you continue to ask questions based upon the answers the person has given you, congratulations, you are now having a conversation with a total stranger. It may seem taxing at first, but with practice it becomes much easier. All you have to do is remember to do your part to aid the budding conversation by giving longer answers, that is, something for the other person to ask about. Also, the beginning of the conversation may be a bit difficult, but if the person seems interested in having a conversation, keep asking questions until you have found common ground.

Gentlemen and ladies, if you are going to an event, *read the sports page*—even if it pains you. Most men have a basic knowledge of sports and can have at least a shallow conversation about sports. The weather page is also good because the weather affects everyone. Compliment the person on their accessories, necklace, jewelry, tie, jacket, shoes, or something that looks interesting to you. If that doesn't lead into a conversation, a good follow-up is *"Where did you get it?"* Most women can talk about fashion and jewelry much better than most men. Of course these are general assumptions, so take them with a "grain of salt." A little bit of sports knowledge and little bit of fashion knowledge will provide ample topics to discuss with a wide range of people. Avoid topics such as politics and religion! These are very polarizing topics.

It is always better to have a positive spin on your questions rather than a negative one, for example, *"Hot enough for ya?"* versus *"This heat reminds me of the time I lived in West Texas. Have you been to the desert?"* In the second example you have also provided some details about your life for the other person to ask you about. This creates an invitation to further conversation—small talk!

This chapter is only an introduction to learning to make small talk. If you have already honed this skill, then, you are one step ahead. If you still need to work on this skill, pick up some good books about small talk.

> *They* [natural introverts] *have practiced, attended seminars, hired personal coaches, and read books. You don't think so? Trust me, I know. I used to be a geeky, introverted engineer—no one has worse skills than I once did. I became a pro by learning the skills and then practicing them. It's that simple.*

> —Debra Fine, <u>The Fine Art of Small Talk</u>

Starter Questions

1. The old standby: How's the weather/wind/rain/heat? Did you get the opportunity to enjoy the beautiful weather today?

2. Another old standby: So what do you do? *You can answer this question with your elevator speech (discussed later).*

3. Did you see that the stock market was up/down today?

4. That is a beautiful necklace/dress/tie, where did you get it?

5. If jewelry looks antique: That broche looks antique, is there a story behind it?

6. How do you think [your local football, baseball, basketball] team is going to do this year? *Following your local team is a good way to always be ready for conversation.*

7. This is a beautiful venue, have you been here before?

8. Have you taken any interesting trips lately?

Exercise

1. Notice something about the next five strangers you interact with in which you could compliment them about.

Challenge

1. Compliment someone on their accessories once a day for a week, e.g. *"That is a good looking tie,"* or *"That is a beautiful necklace."*

2. Talk with someone new every day. It doesn't have to be a deep conversation, just small talk with a complete stranger. The grocery store is a great place to start.

3. Meet two new people. Get a name and swap business cards. Then follow up and have coffee with one or both of them.

Chapter 2

Going Up: Develop Your Elevator Speech

"It says 'best-selling author', not best 'writing author'."

—Robert Kiyosaki, <u>Rich Dad Poor Dad</u>

I often meet people at work and around town, and one common question is, *"So what do you do?"*

The first few times I tried to answer this question I fumbled around trying to come up with something that told the person everything about what I did at my job. Sometimes I rambled on and on for several minutes; sometimes I gave a short, half-sentence answer in three seconds. The former bored the person, and the latter didn't tell them anything. Somewhere in the middle is the elevator speech.

An elevator speech is **your verbal business** card and a personal advertisement to everyone you meet. It can be memorable, brief, and politely convey all the necessary information, or it can be ineffective by being too short or long-winded. This is the first impression the other person will have of you. Make it a lasting, positive impression. Make it a sale!

What is an elevator speech? Loosely defined (there are many definitions and descriptions); an elevator speech is a 30-second, two- to four-sentence blurb about yourself. This is just enough to tell someone all about you in the time it takes to go between floors on an elevator. As a budding expert communicator, it's important to leave enough time to hear the other person's elevator speech too. You might want to develop a couple of different elevator speeches for use depending on your audience. I am a highly trained scientist, and the elevator speech I use at work is not the same elevator speech I use when I meet people at my kid's school. Industry-specific jargon and acronyms are great when you are interacting with people in your industry, but it will only confuse (and possibly alienate) people outside of your industry. Develop two or three elevator speeches, think about when and where to use each one and try them out on friends and family who are familiar with your subject matter.

There are five key elements to an effective elevator speech:

1. Be succinct: You only have a short time (literally and figuratively) to engage the other person and to grab their attention.

2. What are you? I did not say "State your job title" because many people, myself included, prefer to be defined by more than just a job title. *"I am a manager at a Fortune 500 company,"* or *"I am the CEO of my own business."*

3. What do you do? What does your company do? *"I make widgets,"* *"I develop new ways to manufacture widgets."*

4. Why do you do this? *"Our widgets are the best in the world, they are used in 90% of gadgets manufactured,"* or *"I love my job because we have great widgets."*

5. State your personal distinction: What is unique about you? Since this is your elevator speech and your advertisement, it should be focused on you. *"I designed the way our widgets interact with the world's gadgets."*

This is one simple formula for an effective elevator speech and is a good beginning. I encourage you to play around with several formulas until you develop an effective speech that you are proud to tell anyone.

Now it is time to begin crafting your elevator speech in more detail. Short speeches are some of the hardest to give because everything has to be worded succinctly and effectively to get your point across. You don't have time to blah blah a description about your widget like you would if you had a captive audience for an hour. Take the formula from the previous paragraph; write out all of the important points, and don't worry about being succinct at this point.

- What are you?

  o *I am the chief widget maker at WAM enterprises.*

- What do you do? What does your company do?

  o *I oversee our team of seven people who develop new widgets and tweak our old widgets to make them more effective at widgeting.*

- Why do you do this?

  o *Our widgets are used in manufacturing of 90% of the gadgets in the world.*

- What is unique about you?

  o *I helped develop our proprietary process that makes our widgets 50% more effective than our competitors.*

Now if we put all of this together and add an introduction we end up with something like this:

Hi, I'm John, the chief widget maker at WAM enterprises. I oversee our team of seven people who develop new widgets and tweak old widgets to make them more effective at widgeting. Our widgets are used in manufacturing 90% of the gadgets in the world. I helped develop our proprietary process that makes our widgets 50% more effective than our competitors.

With a little rearrangement we now have:

Hi, I'm John, the chief widget maker at WAM enterprises overseeing our team of seven people. Our team develops new widgets and tweaks old widgets to make them more effective at widgeting. I helped develop our proprietary process that makes our widgets 50% more effective than our competitors, allowing us to gain a 90% market share in the use of widgets for manufacturing.

This is a good start for a general elevator speech. Details can be added when you are talking to people in the industry, such as the specific name of the widget and how it is used in manufacturing.

Dan Miller, author and career coach, has developed a similar model that is a bit more achievement-focused and ends with a call to action:

- What problem does my expertise solve?

- What in my background has prepared me for being excellent in this area?

- Here's a specific time when I used those skills.

- Call to action: Here's how my skills would fit in here.

Using this model, we come up with another iteration of our elevator speech:

> *Hi, I'm John, and I am the chief widget maker at WAM Enterprises. We make the widgets used in the production of gadgets. I oversee our team in the development of new widgets and with our new designs our widgets are 50% more effective than our competitors and have increased our market share by 90%. For example, the new gadgets being produced today, such as this new cell phone, all use our new proprietary widgets. Do you know anyone who needs to increase manufacturing efficiency?*

Did you notice how this one ended with a general call to action and asked about increased manufacturing efficiency, not just manufacturing involving widgets? More general questions open the door to larger audiences, and the focus is on efficiency instead of widgets.

If you have developed a good elevator speech, the conversation will immediately begin flowing. You have left the person wanting to learn more about you and what you do. You have also given them ample information to formulate questions to get the details they are interested in. The person you just gave your speech to may use your widgets everyday and may have a great idea for tweaking them. They may use the product that the widgets are used to manufacture, or they may not know anything about widgets or even care. But a good elevator speech will spark their interest. If your speech constantly produces "glassy-eyed" looks or never brings any questions, it is time to go back to the drawing board and rework your speech. If your speech leads to questions, conversations, and the passing of business cards, you know that you have an effective elevator speech!

Exercises

1. Develop a general elevator speech. Play with additional templates. Start with a longer version and reword it to create a succinct and effective elevator speech.

2. Alter the elevator speech from the first exercise:

   a. Add details including industry-specific jargon, and try it out on coworkers.

   b. Remove details so people outside of the industry can understand it and think your job is really cool. Try it out on your mother, your significant other, your neighbors, and your kids. If they get that "glassy-eyed" look, go back to the drawing board.

3. Listen to as many elevator speeches as you can in the next week, and pay particular attention to what intrigues you and why? What did the person say that makes you want to ask a question? What bores you and why? What was unclear or confusing about the other person?

Challenge

1. Give each of your speeches to two or three people this week.

2. Pay particular attention to how it sounds and the reactions from the listener: Are they bored or interested? Did your elevator speech inspire follow-up questions or was the response pat response of, "that's nice"?

Section II

Gaining Confidence

Believing something is possible is the first step in taking action towards achieving a goal.

Chapter 3

Finding Your Confidence

A man is literally what he thinks, his character being the complete sum of all his thoughts.

—James Allen, <u>As a Man Thinketh</u>

Truly, "thoughts are things," and powerful things at that, when they are mixed with definiteness of purpose, persistence, and a burning desire for their translation into riches, or other material objects.

—Napoleon Hill, <u>Think and Grow Rich</u>

When I first started reading the works of Napoleon Hill and James Allen, I thought all of this mumbo-jumbo about "thinking it makes it happen" was misguided. After all, if I thought I was a millionaire and acted like one, I would still have the same amount of money and would still drive the same car. If I thought I was successful in business, I still had the same job at the same pay. After a few months of letting these readings sink in, I finally understood the great insight these writers had. If I think I am successful and act successful, *I will begin doing things that will lead to success.* If I want to be a millionaire I have to believe it is possible. Believing something is possible is the first step in taking action towards achieving a goal.

Confidence is a key factor in having the courage to stand up in front of a crowd of strangers and present material as the expert. Fear of rejection and the possibility of falling short destroy our self-confidence. These fears create one giant pothole in our ability to be comfortable in front of any crowd. However, this crowd of strangers does not want to listen to a long boring talk, they want to listen to a great talk filled with lots of useful and exciting information. **They want you to succeed!** These strangers are already your supporters.

Very early in my graduate-school days, I received some sage advice while preparing for one of my first talks. I was young, just out of college, and was preparing to talk to a roomful of world-class scientists with Ph.D.s and M.D.s about the work I had been doing over the past year. I was scared and nervous: What if these experts didn't like it? What if they thought I was an idiot? What if I tripped? What if I froze on stage? What if I forgot my words? What if, what if… Every horrible scenario and Murphy's Law event that I could imagine went through my head. During one practice session, my mentor at the time gave me this piece of wisdom that I have since passed along to countless people.

> *"This is your project; you know more about this project than anyone else in the entire world, including me."*
>
> —Bob Radinsky, Ph.D.

It took a minute, but I soon realized he was right. This was my project; I knew it better than anyone because I worked on it every day. These people were coming from all over the world to hear me—not the guy next door, me! They believed I had something of value to share with them, and they didn't know anything about me. Yes, there were people in the audience who might know parts of the project better, like how A fits into B, but I was the expert in how my project, my talk, was produced, and how the data and details were interpreted. My stage may have been small and the scope tiny in the grand scheme of things; but, for the moment, *I was the expert.*

You are an expert on the topic you have been asked to present. Most likely, there was a chain of events that led to you personally being asked to give a presentation, beginning with someone recognizing that you were the go to guy. It may have gone something like this:

John: *Hi, Sue. I would like to learn more about how these widgets are made.*

Sue: *That is a great idea, John. We use these widgets every day, but I don't know anything about them. Why don't you ask around and see if someone in our company knows anything about them.*

John [an hour later]: *No one here seems to know much about these widgets, Sue. Maybe we should contact the company who makes them. I will call WAM enterprises.*

John [on the phone with a person at WAM enterprises]: *Hi, we use your widgets in our manufacturing process, but we don't know anything about them. Do you have someone you can send to our headquarters to tell us all about these widgets?*

WAM Enterprises: *Sure, John. We have a great guy who is an expert in all things widget. I will have him call and schedule a time to give you a widget seminar.*

John: *Thanks. I look forward to learning all about widgets— the new knowledge will really help our company understand our processing.*

In other words, you have been chosen to give a talk because you have special knowledge that is desired by the receiver. John did not walk up to a random stranger on the street and ask for a talk on widgets; he went straight to the source,

WAM Enterprises. In turn, WAM Enterprises wants to send out a qualified person to impart knowledge upon John and his team. WAM Enterprises has chosen the best person for the job, someone they consider an expert in the field. You were chosen because your peers value your knowledge and feel you are an expert. If you have been asked to give a presentation and you don't feel you are an expert on the subject, you are selling yourself short. The fact that you have been asked means that you are considered an expert.

Think confidently, and you will be confident.

Exercises

1. Think and believe confidently.

2. Give yourself daily positive affirmations.

3. Identify areas in your life that are sabotaging your ability to think confidently.

   a. Yourself: Are you your own worst enemy?

   b. Spouse: Is he or she your champion or your detractor?

   c. Life situation: Have you been "knocked down"?

Challenge

1. Look around at your environment and identify areas in which you are an expert.

2. What advice do people seek from you?

3. What decisions do you make confidently in your career? In your home life?

4. What special skills do you have?

Chapter 4

A Deer in the Headlights

Fears are nothing more than states of mind.

—Napoleon Hill, <u>Think and Grow Rich</u>

There is no greater illusion than fear,

no greater wrong than preparing to defend yourself,

no greater misfortune than having an enemy.

Whoever can see through all fear will always be safe.

—Lao-Tzu, <u>Tao Te Ching</u>

Having grown up in the Midwest, I am all too familiar with the phrase, "… like a deer in the headlights." When you are driving at night, and you come upon a deer standing in the middle of the road, your headlights hit the deer, they stop, look, and sometimes they freeze. This reaction doesn't have very optimistic chances for survival!

This analogy is handy because it so aptly applies to certain people when they are put in front of a crowd. Of course, others thrive in front of crowds—we have all seen them. They seem to pull energy from the crowd, giving fantastic, enthusiastic talks. If you thrive on stage and in front of crowds, this chapter isn't for you. This chapter is designed for those of us who get scared and freeze up when presented with an opportunity to be in the spotlight.

If you plan to give a talk or a live presentation of any kind, you will be in front of people. If you have a fear of being in the spotlight, you have to find ways to "get over it" or at least deal with it. The crowd may be three people or 300, but both will make you nervous.

Unless you are reading your presentation, don't have visual aids, and won't be taking any questions, you will probably have to do some moving, coordinating, and thinking while on stage. We will focus on these skills in later chapters. This chapter is designed to help you begin to feel comfortable in front of an audience.

I did some things in high school and college that I thought were just being a good citizen—giving back to my community. In hindsight I can see how they prepared me to be in the spotlight, even if it was only for a few minutes at a time.

I was a reader at my church. This turned out to be very simple, very easy, yet very effective preparation for public speaking. Once a month, I would stand up in front of the congregation of 400 people and read two to three passages from the Bible or a piece of paper. This required me to read the material beforehand to make sure I could pronounce everything, to put on a tie, to walk to the podium at the right time, to speak clearly into a microphone, and to walk back, all with perfect timing. I was always a little nervous. What if I tripped on the way up? What if I pronounced something incorrectly? What if... Looking back, this was a great way to become comfortable in front large crowds, and also speaking to them. I didn't have to worry about visual aids, moving around on stage, or even thinking. I just walked on, read, and walked off: no thinking, just doing. I gained valuable experience on stage in a way that was minimally stressful because I only had to deal with one issue of live presentations, that is, being the focus of everyone's attention. The more I did it, the more comfortable I became in the spotlight.

Today in our communities, there are many opportunities to get in front of a crowd and just read. The important concept here is to be in front of people without having to think hard or do very many things. Churches, schools, senior centers, and libraries are always looking for people to read. If you have small children, their classrooms are probably the easiest and quickest venues in which to volunteer. If you don't have kids, your friends or relatives do. Taking action to do public reading is a great way to overcome your fears. Now is the time to take action.

After you have been in front of an audience a few times, you will recognize that the likelihood of realizing your worst fears is minimal. You didn't pee your pants, you didn't trip or fall out of your chair, and you weren't standing there naked. Although you might have been acutely aware of that word you missed, the itch in your foot, an occasional mispronunciation, or briefly losing your place on page 23, these are all small mistakes that we all make over and over again. You will learn to ignore them because it is unlikely that your audience even noticed—especially that itch in your foot.

By reading to community organizations, you will gain valuable experience being in front of crowd—all while serving your community.

Challenge

Find an organization and volunteer to read to a group this week. It will probably take at least two or three reading sessions before you gain some self-assurance in your abilities.

Section III

Preparing for Your Presentation

Prior planning prevents poor performance.

Chapter 5

Planning for Your Audience

If you know the enemy and know yourself, you need not fear the result of a hundred battles. If you know yourself but not the enemy, for every victory gained you will also suffer a defeat. If you know neither the enemy nor yourself, you will succumb in every battle.

—Sun Tzu, The Art of War

There is a philosophy called the 5-P philosophy, aptly named because it goes like this, *Prior Planning Prevents Poor Performance.* It makes a great mantra for preparing a live presentation. Proper planning will go a long way in making you look professional and preventing a major disaster.

Your audience is an often overlooked area of preparation, and it should be the place you start. After all, these are the people you will be speaking to and interacting with the entire time. They will be asking questions directly to you. You need to know who they are, what they are about, and why they believe your talk is worth *their* time. In this chapter's introductory quote, Sun Tzu was describing the necessity of knowing your enemy in battle. Of course, a presentation is not a battle that you can win or lose. However, the quote demonstrates the importance of knowing about those with whom you are interacting. If you know your audience, achieving the goals of your presentation will be much easier.

Most of us have seen plenty of presentations that were generic and not tailored to the audience. We all know the importance of taking the time to tailor our resumes for only a few people to read, for example, so why not also tailor each presentation for the audience? Would you talk to a five-year-old the same way you speak to a teenager or to your boss? No! A chemistry talk to business professionals is a waste of everyone's time. You don't want to be the person who wasted one hour of 50 people's lives—that is the equivalent of two entire days!

KNOW YOUR AUDIENCE! SPEAK TO YOUR AUDIENCE!

When I am asked to give a presentation, I spend a lot of time asking about and studying the audience thoroughly. Good sources of information include the person who invited you to speak, any friends in the organization, members of your social network who may be attending, the company's Web page, and Web searches.

Size Matters

The size of your audience makes a big difference in your direct interactions with people. Generally, there is an inverse correlation between the size of the audience and the number of questions asked during a presentation, as demonstrated in the graph below. The number and type of questions asked after the presentation depend upon the individuals in the audience. People in a full auditorium are unlikely to ask you questions during your talk because larger audiences tend to hold questions until the end.

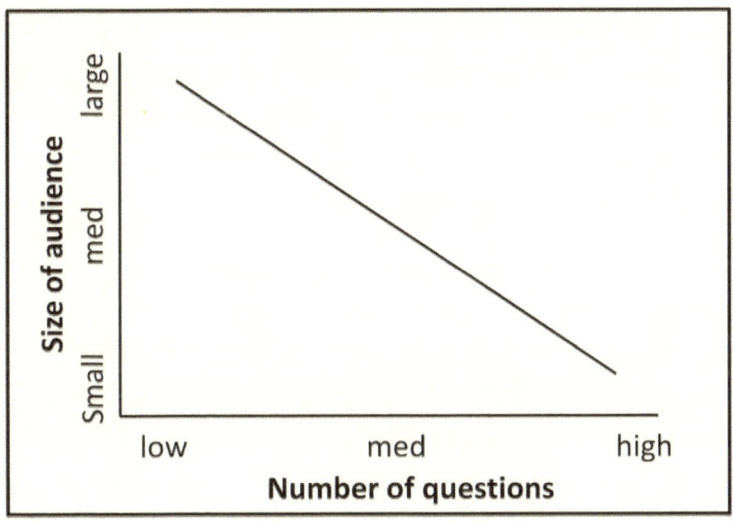

In smaller groups of 8 to 20 (like a classroom setting), people are more comfortable asking questions during your presentation. This is a good-sized group with which to interact because it is small enough to engage individuals but large enough that one audience member usually won't dominate. Audience members will often ask for clarification of points and issues relating to their own work or "the big picture." They may also ask philosophical or general questions about your presentation.

Be prepared for someone to ask a question that leads you on a tangent, and be prepared to redirect it back to your topic. With an audience of this size and smaller, it is important to know who will be in your audience (this is discussed in detail below).

With this size group you will have the opportunity to interact with the audience on your terms. If you wish for them to hold their questions until the end, ask them to do so. If you are comfortable with them asking questions during your talk, let them know. Be aware of yourself and your abilities. Taking questions during your talk may derail your train of thought. You are in charge, and you need to do what works for you.

Groups of less than eight are likely to treat your presentation more like a workshop, with constant interaction between you and them. This is a small enough group that it is possible to interact with everyone, answering questions from each person. This size of group can be a lot of fun, but you need to manage the group if they start to divert you from the topic. With a small group you can also ask members of the audience questions, and you can let them answer each other's questions. This will engage the audience, create a less formal atmosphere, and take some of the spotlight pressure off of you.

Occasionally, you may be asked to participate in a different type of presentation, such as a poster presentation, a tradeshow booth, or at a greeting or host station. Usually these types of presentations require interacting with only one or two people for only a few minutes. Then they move on and the cycle repeats.

This is where your elevator speech experience will come in handy. You will need to have a two- to four-minute prepared speech, and if they want to know more, they will ask. Don't be afraid of the constant questions, you will find that more than 50% of the questions will all be the same, they will just be asked by different people. These interactions can easily end up being a conversation, and your small-talk skills will come in handy here. By paying attention to what the other person is saying or asking, you can formulate great answers and great follow-up questions. Here you will interact with a wide group of people; some will think you are great; some will think you are an idiot. When you encounter someone whom you can never please, don't try. Say, "Thank you for your time," and move along. One-on-one interactions can be very rewarding. In addition to giving valuable information, you can also receive it as well.

Types of Audiences

You will encounter many different types of audiences and it is important to understand who they are and what type of information they are after.

- **Corporate audiences** are generally a group of like-minded individuals who have come together for a common purpose: It may be a group of engineers, CEOs or a community advocacy group. They have gathered for a common purpose: to gain information that will help them meet a common objective. It is important to know who and what they are so your message is crafted appropriately for them.

- **Thought leaders** are experts in their field whom other professionals go to for advice. In some cases you may have one or two thought leaders in your audience, or you may have a room full of them. These people may be some of your more notable audience members as discussed in greater detail below.

- **Influencers** are people who will influence the decisions of others. The most common influencers are friends and family. We have a general inclination to trust the decisions of the people we know, thus, their opinions influence our decisions. Influencers are trusted sources of information such as community or civic groups, online social groups, and advocacy groups. Each has specific areas of expertise and knowledge, and your presentation must be tailored to their needs for maximum effectiveness.

MATCH YOUR MESSAGE TO YOUR AUDIENCE!

Education/Experience

You have been asked to give a presentation to this group to increase their knowledge and experience. You have valuable information that they are seeking and this information needs to be presented in a format they understand. My training has been highly scientific, and I would not give a highly scientific talk, using molecular biology terms, to a group of accountants. Inversely, I would not understand a talk full of accounting jargon—in fact, I would probably fall asleep. Give an engineering talk to engineers, a scientific talk to scientists, and a business talk to business people. If you have to give a business talk to scientific people you will need to remove some of the industry-specific lingo and explain many things that seem basic to you. What seems dumb to you and those in your industry will not seem dumb to people outside of your area of expertise.

Notable People

Often you will have notable audience members. It is in your best interest to know who they are and little bit about them before you arrive. For example, you may be giving a talk about the integration of your widget with X, Y, and Z products, and the world's expert on X will be sitting in your audience. It is important to know who this person is, why they are considered an expert, and how and why they got there. If possible, find out their thoughts on the integration of widgets with X, Y, and Z as well as their thoughts on the integration of X with widgets.

Other types of notable attendees may be company heads (CEOs) or departmental bosses. They could end up being your friends, enemies, next employers, or just audience members. If you have done your homework, you can easily make them your friends by incorporating their work, thoughts, or philosophy into your talk. This shouldn't be the focus of your talk, but you can make a single bullet point that acknowledges their expertise and gives them proper credit. This will show that you are aware of other work in the field, how your widget has built upon previous widgets, and how it fits into the bigger picture. Acknowledging their contributions to the field will give them a sense of pride. A few examples are shown below.

- *"At WAM Enterprises we were looking for ways to make a better widget, and one of your very own engineers, Phil Johnson, had previously designed a fascinating widget that we were able to make a few modifications to so that it would fit our needs."*

- *"Your CEO, Jane Johnson, consistently led a team of great engineers that has revolutionized the widget industry with their creative designs."*

Almost as important as knowing who the notable audience members are, it is also important to know who the notable people are that will be on vacation. If you spend hours researching Jane Johnson's rise to CEO, but she is out of the office for two weeks, your new-found knowledge won't be of much use.

The Internet and company Web sites are great places to begin when looking for this type of information. Once you have a name, you can learn volumes on the Web. Another great place to access resources is the person who asked you to give the presentation. If the world's expert on something related to your topic is going to be in your audience, you should already have known that. However, what you might not know is who will be on vacation. Here's where your contacts at the company can come in handy, and they may divulge the information without your asking. With your new small-talk skills, you should be able to effectively extract some useful information.

Antagonist

We have all seen an antagonist in action in a crowd. If you go to seminars regularly, you probably know them by name and can predict what kinds of questions they will ask. If you give very many presentations, you will probably end up on the receiving end of some of these antagonistic activities. If you are able to find out whom they are beforehand and what types of questions they might ask, you can prepare effective responses.

When I was in graduate school, I had to attend our weekly departmental seminar, and eventually it was my turn to present. After having attended over 50 seminars with generally the same group of people, I knew who the antagonists were and what kinds of questions they would ask. I was able to use this knowledge to my advantage, and I incorporated their questions into my talk. They asked antagonistic questions, and I had the answers on the next slide! I looked like a genius, and they were a little embarrassed. Their adversarial attitudes did not continue with me.

It can be useful to understand an individual's motivations for being adversarial. A few reasons for antagonism and ideas for dealing with them are shown below.

- Just likes a good argument

    If the person just likes a good argument, they are just having fun, and you should have fun too with this type of antagonist. You can direct and guide these questions back to your topic of focus fairly easily with a little practice and adequate knowledge of your topic.

- Wants you to know how smart they are

- Wants the audience to know how smart they are

    With these two reasons, the antagonist has an internal need to look good in front of his or her home crowd. This type of antagonist is easily disarmed with a little knowledge beforehand. Simply incorporate his or her name and work into your talk, and the antagonist has achieved the goal of looking smart in front of their peers and colleagues.

- Does not agree with you

    If your antagonist just simply does not agree with you, it is vital to understand why. You can acquire this knowledge beforehand by doing some homework, or during your talk by asking the antagonist questions. If you have done your homework beforehand, you can incorporate this opposing viewpoint into your presentation, such as "a differing opinion on widgets exists and it is…" This demonstrates that you are aware of the differing opinion and have not cast it aside as unworthy of consideration. Being open-minded is a difficult but highly valuable skill. If you need to acquire this information during your talk, you can ask a few questions of your antagonist and then accept it as a valid viewpoint followed by an explanation of why you have chosen a differing opinion. This is the most productive response to this common type of antagonist and is least likely to perpetuate an adversarial interaction. Occasionally, however, you will find one that is very difficult to impede. Be patient, firm, kind, and move on!

- Does not like you

    When someone just doesn't like you and wants to be adversarial during your talk, they will find any reason to be a jerk. Try to keep the topic on focus, and don't let them divert you from your topic—it won't end well for you. You are on their home turf.

If this type of antagonist continues, you may need to tell them they are being a jerk in front of the entire audience. Of course you would not say, *"Stop it, you jerk,"* but it is acceptable to say something like:

- *"Let's hold anymore questions until the end."*

- *"For the sake of the rest of the audience, let's get back to the topic at hand."*

- *"I see we aren't getting anywhere, so let's agree to disagree."*

- *"I would be happy to discuss this with you afterwards."*

Gentle redirection won't often work with this type of antagonist, and you need to be blunt. If this type of antagonist continues, as a last resort, you may find it helpful to ask them what his or her objective is in front of the entire audience.

You are on stage and in charge; don't hesitate to exert some executive power once in a while. After all, the people came to hear what you have to say, not to hear you argue with one person.

Friends and Enemies

Who are your friends and who are your enemies in the audience? Your friends may literally be your friends—the

40

guys you watch football with, go to dinner and a movie with—or they may figuratively be your friends, such as associates you met at a conference last year, colleagues who share similar philosophies about the industry, etc. Your enemies will be those with opposing viewpoints or that one guy who just doesn't like you. The more friends you have in the audience, the more comfortable you will be. Your friends can help you by answering an occasional question (that you didn't know), or they can help you redirect the antagonist. Friends are also a great source of information as discussed in the following sections.

Finding the Information

When you are invited to give a presentation, the person contacting you is a great place to start asking questions about the audience: How big will the audience be? Who will be there? What is the focus? Probe this person for as much information as you can get without being annoying. You may be contacted by a secretary or administrative assistant. They can be valuable resources and provide you with a tremendous amount of information and direction. Just think about what they control: access to people, updates, and messages; the practical knowledge of a "first point of contact" person. Don't ever underestimate the person answering the phone! If they like you, the entire company will be at your fingertips. Administrative assistants control schedules, and they talk to each other. They will know who is on vacation or out of town. A friend may be able to warn you about potential antagonists or help you anticipate the CEO or other noteworthy attendees. But it is unlikely that your friends will know who has scheduled a vacation for that week—the administrative assistants will. Your small-talk skills, being nice, and saying "Please" and "Thank you" will go a long way with everyone.

If you have literal friends, they will be the greatest source of information. They can tell you about the antagonists, your figurative friends, and your figurative enemies—and their potential motives. They may even be able to tell you what types of questions people will ask and about the behaviors and dynamics of the audience. You can learn a lot if you have a literal friend who is willing to sit down and talk with you.

Associates can also be great sources of information, but they are not likely to open up quite as much. They are less likely to stick their neck out and give opinions and more likely to keep things factual. During my graduate-school days I worked with many people just prior to committee meetings; we used our extensive network of students to find out exactly what types of questions would be asked and by whom. These students could predict with amazing accuracy the exact questions that would be asked by the professor for whom they worked. By working daily with the professor, they were able to understand and predict his or her thought processes. Having this knowledge allowed many people to develop high-quality, complete answers to these questions prior to giving their talks.

The Internet and company Web sites are great places to begin looking for information. Once you have a name, you can find volumes of information on the Web about a person's history, expertise, rise to power, and usually even some extracurricular activities and volunteer organizations.

The Internet is a great place to start and can offer many facts, but it is a terrible place to end your information gathering. Using your small-talk skills can help you leverage your contacts to divulge information that is not available on company Web sites.

Exercises

1. Ask your friends about the audiences in their offices. Find out who the antagonists are, who the notable people are, what the experience of the group is, who attends seminars. With practice and experience you will get better at asking questions about your audience.

2. Pay attention to the audience in the next seminar you attend. If you don't have one scheduled, seek one out. The topic is irrelevant; sit in the back and pay attention to the audience. How many people are there? What are they doing? How many are sleeping, texting, or taking notes? We will cover these topics in later chapters.

3. Attend seminars with large groups and small groups, compare and contrast the audience sizes and their interaction with the speaker.

Chapter 6

Content: The Devil Is in the Details, or Lack Thereof...

> *A philosophy can and must be worked out with the greatest rigour and discipline in the details, but can ultimately be founded on nothing but faith: and this is the reason, I suspect, why the novelties in philosophy are only in elaboration, and never in fundamentals.*
>
> —T. S. Eliot, <u>Knowledge and Experience in the Philosophy of F. H. Bradley</u>

"The devil is in the details." We have all heard this phrase, usually in regard to some legal document or contract of some kind. I took the liberty of adding "or lack thereof..." to it. What do I mean by this? When writing a paper or having a conversation with a person, you have the freedom to include lots and lots of details; however, when giving a presentation with aids such as slides or a poster, you don't have this luxury. There is a fine line between too much detail and too little. On a PowerPoint slide, you can supply three or four bullet points but not a paragraph of writing. Effectively using this limited space will significantly enhance your speaking skills too. In this chapter we will discuss the content and layout of your presentation aids.

We are going to focus on live presentations with slide shows as visual aids. There are many other types of live presentations that you may encounter, and many of these techniques are applicable to other types of presentations. However, here we are focusing on presentations for a typical talk involving multiple slides. When crafting your presentation, it is important to note that visual aids are great for pictures and graphs but terrible for words. Conversely, speaking is great for words but not-so-great for describing a picture. Incorporate both techniques into your speaking style.

We begin with a general layout as shown in the figure below.

Slide Title
- Content
- Content
- Content

Slide Summary

Reference/slide credit

While this is a very simple slide, it is a general template and a good place to start. By no means is it the only style to use. In fact, as you gain more experience, I encourage you to try variations of this layout and add your own personal touches. Web searches and PowerPoint itself will provide access to numerous additional templates. Also, pay attention to other talks you attend. These will all give you great ideas for layout and content—what to include and what to avoid! Experiment with different things; see what works well for you, your audience, and your content.

Size Matters

A discussion about presentations would not be complete without a discussion of font size. If your font size is too small, your audience won't be able to see it. If it is too large, you won't be able to provide much information on your slide. However, the proper font size will also be determined by the size of your room and audience. A large room, where the audience is 100 feet away, will require a larger font than a small room where the participants are 10 feet away. In addition to the size of the room, you should also consider the audience and their potential range of sight. A group likely to have poor eyesight will need a larger font than a group more likely to have good eyesight. The size of the room is a question you will want to ask when you are researching your audience.

Generally, font sizes between 18 and 44 points are great to use. Never use a font size smaller than 14 points; it will be just too small, and only those audience members with extremely good eyesight or those sitting right up front will be able to see it. Just think of your own reaction if you decided to spend an hour listening to a speaker only to find out that you are unable to read any of the slides. Make a slide like the one below; find a room of a similar size and see how well you can read these different font sizes from various parts of the room. If you can't read it from the back of the room, odds are that your audience won't be able to read it either. This exercise will be very enlightening.

This is 12 point font
This is 14 point font
This is 16 point font
This is 18 point font
This is 20 point font
This is 24 point font
This is 28 point font
This is 32 point font

In addition to font size, we need to consider font styles. Compare Times New Roman and Arial.

- This font is Times New Roman.
- This font is Arial.

Times New Roman is a serif-type font, meaning it has "smaller lines used to finish off a main stroke of a letter," whereas Arial is a sans-serif-type font, meaning without serifs. When reading from a typed page, serif-type fonts work well, but a sans-serif font works better when reading from a computerized image. You can also choose a font that works with your personal style such as a more formal font or a less formal and fun font such as comic sans. Just make sure that it is easy to read from the back of the room.

Color Matters

Color choice plays a large role in how your audience subconsciously perceives your presentation and their ability to see it. For instance, a presentation filled with lots of bright colors such as reds, hot pinks, and bright oranges will leave your audience feeling slightly agitated. In contrast, a presentation filled with warm soothing colors such as blues and golds will help to evoke a calming sensation. However, using these bright colors to highlight a few words can be a very effective tool when used judiciously.

Start with a calm background color such as blue or white, and then choose a highly contrasting color for the fonts. Black font on a white background is one of the most contrasting color schemes you will find, but it is also a boring color scheme. Try gold fonts on a blue background or green fonts on a purple background. You can find some great discussions of color schemes on Microsoft's Website, and I recommend reading the online article referenced in the *"References and Further Reading"* section. The predefined color schemes in PowerPoint have been tested and analyzed for maximal effectiveness. There are hundreds of available templates, and they are a great place to start. As you gain more confidence and experience, adjust the color schemes and templates to fit your personal needs and style.

Be Consistent

Remaining consistent throughout your presentation makes things easier to understand and allows your audience to follow you more easily. First, in terms of layout, each slide should use a similar color and font scheme such as a blue background with gold Arial font. Rarely change backgrounds and fonts. If you change them too often, your audience will be paying attention to the background and format changes and not the content of the slide. Second, use the same nomenclature throughout your talk. For instance, don't call it a widget in one slide, capitalize Widget in another, and abbreviate widg. in a third. Pick one name and stay with it. Consistency enables your audience to pay attention to your content and not the constant changes—always review your slides for consistency.

Title

This is the introduction to your slide; it sets the stage and tone for the content of your slide. Since the title will be at the top of your slide and will summarize your slide, it should be the largest font on the slide: a 32 to 44-point font works well. Succinct, efficient titles require practice, and everyone gets better with time. The importance of a good title cannot be understated. *If your audience reads one thing on your slide, it will be the title.* If it bores them, they will tune out. If they are intrigued, you will have their undivided attention. Spend a significant amount of time on your titles. Write them, read them, rework them, and write them again until they accurately summarize the slides in an exciting manner. When you think you have great titles, run them by other people and get their input. If they are confused, your audience will probably be confused, too.

You should convey as much information as possible into each title. It takes practice to say who, what, when, where and how in ten words or less! Ten words may seem drastically brief, but the title should summarize all of the content that will be presented on your slide. For example, if your slide is going to convince me that widgets from WAM Enterprises are the best widgets for the manufacturing of gadgets, your title might read, "The best widgets for making gadgets" or "WAM's widgets are great for making gadgets." Compare those direct titles with ambiguous titles like "Widgets and gadgets" or "Widgets are used to make gadgets." The latter two titles really don't say anything of value, and they only tell the audience that widgets and gadgets will be discussed in the slide. If your slide focuses on the cost benefit of using WAM's widgets, the title might read "Cost savings of WAM widgets" or "Our widgets save you money," or to accountants, "The cost–benefit ratio of WAM widgets." With these titles I have stated the following:

- Who: *WAM Enterprises doing business with you*

- What: *WAM Enterprises widgets* (as compared to our competitor's widgets)

- When: *As soon as you begin using them*

- Where: *Your company*

- How: *By using them in your company you will save money*

With this title, I have not given away specific details but I have whet the audience's appetite for the details of how our widgets are great. The details will follow in the slide's content.

Content

This section is the "meat," the "nuts and bolts," the details of the slide. This section is where you get into more detail about why WAM Enterprises' widgets are the best. There are many ways to convey this to your audience: testimonials, pictures, charts, graphs, numbers, and examples, just to name a few. Here you must decide how much content to put on a slide. Too much information will be hard to follow, and too little will waste space. However, it is always better to err on the side of less content rather than trying to cram more content onto the slide.

- Typically three to four bullet points of one to two lines each are the maximum. Any more and you might as well be writing a paragraph. These bullet points should supply only the necessary details in writing. Use your words to fill in the gaps and to provide additional details and explanations. Bullet points can be used to provide testimonials, written examples, and numbers.

- A picture says a thousand words, as the old saying goes. Adding pictures to your presentation can help to show your audience how your widget fits into the manufacturing schema. Many intricate explanations can be avoided with a simple picture. You can even combine a few pictures to show a time line or to compare different widgets. Be sure to label your pictures appropriately so that your audience knows what it is without having to listen to you or to ask you. I have often been in the middle of a talk and was unable to remember exactly what the picture shows. Having it properly and completely labeled will avoid this mishap. With a picture you can also include a couple of bullet points to help describe it and to "jog" your memory when discussing the slide.

- If you need to show complex data in a simple, easy-to-view format, a graph may be your best option. With a properly made graph you can show and compare different concepts in an easy-to-read format. Use thick lines with dark colors on the graph as thin lines are not easily seen. If you don't have exact data, you may consider making a graph to illustrate the point. Just be sure your audience knows that the graph isn't real.

After you have presented the graph, you can highlight certain parts by inserting a circle, oval, or square to cover your most interesting points. As with all content, only do this a maximum of two to three times per graph.

If your graph is simple and easy to understand, it is acceptable to add a few bullet points or a second comparison graph on the same slide. However, if your graph is complicated, then <u>absolutely do not</u> add any more content than necessary to make the point of the slide. Remember to consider your graph from the eyes of your audience; they will see it differently than you do. After all, you are the expert in this topic.

- Tables are a great way to present a tremendous amount of data in a very succinct format. Organize the table in the order you will discuss it, from left to right, and be sure there is not so much data that the font is too small for the audience to read. Just like a graph, you may have a few points you wish to highlight; this can be done by changing the font color, bolding, italics, underlining, or circling.

However, try not to use more than two or three different ways to highlight your data. For example, don't make one column bold, a second column yellow, one row green, and another row in italics. It will begin to look like a confusing cartoon. Use highlighting sparingly, and it will become a strong tool during your presentation. Because tables usually contain a tremendous amount of data, don't add multiple tables or bullet points on the same slide unless absolutely necessary.

- Using animation is a great way to show your content in parts. You may be asking, "What is slide show animation?" This is a way in which only parts of your slide will show up each time you advance the slide. For example, you may wish to show a picture of your widget and have your audience focus on the overall widget, followed by having arrows point at particular parts of the widget as you describe each one. This will highlight one piece without allowing the other parts to detract from what you are currently talking about.

In these slide show programs there are literally thousands of animation combinations that can be used during your presentation. I have seen talks in which the presenter tried to use all of the different types of animations just because he could: it gave me a headache and was hard to follow. Just because you can doesn't mean you should! If you want to use animation, choose one style and stick with it. Also, I would not recommend that beginners use lots of animations. I have often forgotten about an animation on a slide. When you forget that you have animated a slide, it is impossible to hide.

Summary

A summary at the end of the slide is optional, but a well-worded title will also include the summary section. After you have created the title and content section, decide whether the slide easily, accurately, and clearly conveys the message you wanted to get across with that particular slide. If not, the summary is your chance to clearly state the purpose for the slide. When slides are full of text, a summary is generally not necessary; however, if your slide has a table, graph, or picture, a summary statement may be warranted to clarify the exact point you wish to make. A summary statement should be no more than two lines long (preferably one line), and the font should be larger than the font size used in the content section but smaller than the title font.

References/Credit for the Slide

Most slides will not require this section, but occasionally you will want to borrow a slide from a friend, use an already published picture, or copy someone else's graph. When this happens, you will need to give the person credit. If what you are showing has been published, you will need to cite the person's name and where and when it was published. If the information has not been published but was given to you by a friend or colleague, you are not legally obligated to tell your audience the author of the slide, but it is an ethical and nice thing to do. Always give credit where credit is due.

Tips for Making a Slide

- Font size should be between 18 and 44 points. Never use anything smaller than 14-point type.

- Err on the side of less content.

- Use animation sparingly.

- Highlight important things with circles or by changing the color (used judiciously).

- Choose a color scheme that provides optimal contrast between the words and the background.

- Be consistent; use the same color scheme and layout on all slides.

- Visual aids are great for picture, graphs, and tables but not for words

My initial reaction to the quote from T.S. Eliot was *"Huh?"* After three or four readings, I was finally able to distill some meaning from it. The first phrase encompasses the importance of this particular chapter, using great rigor and discipline in the details. Careful selection of words and phrases will make your presentation clear and concise; however, big flowery words and too much detail will leave your audience needing to read your slides three or four times to understand their meaning.

Chapter 7

Organizing Your Talk

There is a kind of genius in a system which can perform apparent wonders with ease. A systematic man can get through so great a quantity of work in such a short time, and with such freedom from exhaustion, as to appear almost miraculous.

—James Allen, As a Man Thinketh

Your organizational skills are crucial in creating a smooth flowing talk. A well-thought-out and organized presentation is easier for you, the speaker, and makes more sense to your audience. You do not want to appear disorganized in your thoughts and ideas. You will lose your audience, literally and figuratively.

There is an old public-speaking adage that anyone who has taken speech in college can recite: Tell them what you are going to tell them, tell them, and then tell them what you told them. A well-organized talk can accomplish this goal without making it obvious that you have taken a page directly from your college public-speaking textbook.

Title Slide

Your talk should always start out with a title slide. This introduces you and your talk to the audience. Just like the titles discussed in the previous chapter, this title needs to accurately describe your presentation. Here you will not be able to describe every idea so focus on the "big picture" or the most exciting idea in your talk. You want to pique your audience's interest with your title. The second section of this slide should be your name, thus introducing you to the audience.

Many people like to put the date and the place the presentation was given next. These should all be in fonts of decreasing size with the title being the largest, the name much smaller, and so on. Most companies you are representing will ask (or require) that you put their logo, picture, and name on the bottom of the slide. Many people also place a small picture of something personal, such as their new baby as inspiration for their work or the beautiful view outside their office window. This can personalize your talk and may help the audience identify with you, but use this technique carefully—avoid religious or political pictures.

Background

The background section should be a review of what is out there in the world that was used as a foundation for your work and presentation. This is the section where you include quotes and ideas from the notable people in your audience. But only do it once or twice; anything more will appear to be obvious brown-nosing. Here you need to describe all of the background information necessary for the audience to understand why WAM Enterprises decided to make a new widget. This includes the current state of widgets, the problem your widgets are fixing, widgets in manufacturing, and the gadgets made using widgets. Depending on the length of your talk, each one of these elements may require their own slide or they may be combined. All of the different types of content described in the previous chapter may be used here in a manner that best illustrates your point.

The Reason for Your Talk

One slide with only two to three lines should contain the reason for your talk. In it you will clearly state why you are giving this talk and what you hope to accomplish. For example, you may wish to have a slide that states something like this: *"Previous widgets were inefficient and were easily broken; our newly redesigned widgets increase productivity and reduce costs."* In science, this would be a hypothesis slide.

This slide summarizes the previous background section and sets the stage for the remainder of your talk. You are now going to show the audience how new widgets from WAM Enterprises will increase productivity and reduce costs.

Content of the Talk

This section will be the bulk of your presentation. Here you will build YOUR story upon the foundation laid in the background. Start with an organized, flowing outline. Each slide should have one point to make and should build upon those that precede it. Clearly state the main idea in the title of the slide, and then fill in the details in the slide content section.

When done properly, this will lead you directly into the next point on the next slide. Continue this theme from slide to slide until all of your points have been made. For example, in the background you described how the old widgets are inefficient and expensive. You would not want to begin the content section of your talk by telling your audience that your new widgets will save them money without telling them first about the old widgets; how your widgets have been redesigned, how this redesign affects the manufacturing, and how the manufacturing of gadgets is made more efficient. This naturally leads into the cost savings idea. A good outline will help you identify an effective progression for your ideas.

Think about your slide show as an assembly line. You would not put the wheels on a car without first putting on the axle, and you can't put the axle on without having a frame to attach it to. This is a progression that needs to build upon itself.

Conclusion

It is a good idea to end the slide show with one or two slides summing up what was said in the content section. In this way, your audience will be reminded, for example, why WAM Enterprises widgets are better than all the others. Bullet three to five of your main points. Try not to use more than five; you don't need to summarize everything. But it is okay to add a little bit of detail here just to remind the audience of the finer points you presented.

Summary

A final summary slide will pull the presentation together and remind them of why you are here and what they have learned. The conclusion slide shows details and particulars of your talk, but a summary slide will show your audience the bigger picture. For example, the conclusion slide stated how the new widgets will save money, but the summary slide will be more basic. For example, it will state *"WAM Enterprises new widgets will revolutionize the gadget manufacturing industry."* This shows a more global overview of WAM Enterprises new widgets and the impact they will have on manufacturing.

Collaboration

Your presentation is a two-way street. You were asked to give a talk because you have information the audience wants or needs, and you agreed to give the talk because the audience also has something you want, such as information, company secrets, manufacturing capabilities, widget buyers, sellers, capital, etc. You hope to gain something out of this presentation; otherwise you would not have agreed to do it. You probably already know what your audience hopes to gain from this talk; it is okay to gently show your audience what you hope to gain and how everyone can work together. If WAM Enterprises is a new startup company, and the audience is filled with potential investors, then you will need to give your audience numbers about how much money they will need to invest, how much they will potentially make, and the timeframe allowed. Your audience may be looking for a brand new widget for the new gadget they plan to start manufacturing next year, and you must tell them what WAM Enterprises wants and is willing to do.

- WAM Enterprises is willing to supply three free widgets.

- We will work with you to design the perfect widget for your new gadget.

- We will provide special financing a guaranteed order of three hundred widgets.

If your goal is a new widget design, new sale, or capital, show your audience how your presentation and two companies working together will be beneficial for both. You may wish to include this section following the summary slide or at the end of the content section. Try it in both places and see which arrangement flows better.

Acknowledgments

No man is an island. Rarely do we work alone, and the people we work with need to receive credit for their efforts. Some of them may be sitting in the audience—I have seen many relationships soured because a speaker forgot to mention the efforts of another. This is sad and can be easily avoided. Another benefit of acknowledging those who have helped us is simple networking. You never know who is connected to whom. Your main collaborator may be the best friend of a notable person in the audience.

Ending Early

I have given, and attended, countless talks that went *waaaayyyy* over the allotted time. Sometimes the speaker did not plan appropriately, and sometimes the audience was so intrigued and asked so many questions that the allotted time was inadequate. With proper planning, you can avoid the first situation; however, when the second problem occurs you have usually captivated the audience and are having a highly constructive interaction with them.

To address this potential situation I like to plan an optional premature stopping point in my talk. Usually this is placed about two-thirds of the way through and can save 15 to 20 minutes from an hour long talk if needed. This is a place where you can end your talk without losing the "meat" of your presentation. If your time is running over, you can skip ahead and bring your presentation to a conclusion. In your conclusions slide you will have a bullet point describing the skipped slides, thus you will be able present the conclusions from the skipped slides but not the content. If your audience has been intrigued and you have to skip slides, you are likely to be asked to return in the future. Building in a premature stopping point won't be noticed if you are on time; however, it will be appreciated if you run long, and you will appear significantly more professional.

Exercises

1. Make an outline of your current work. See how it flows; rearrange it; see if it flows better or worse; and determine why.

2. Develop a title for your work that both encompasses the important points and piques the interest of your audience so that they will want to ask further questions.

Chapter 8

Be Prepared

No one is so brave that he is not disturbed by something unexpected.

—Julius Caesar

Now the general who wins a battle makes many calculations in his temple ere the battle is fought. The general who loses a battle makes but few calculations beforehand. Thus do many calculations lead to victory, and few calculations to defeat: how much more no calculations at all! It is by attention to this point that I can foresee who is likely to win or lose.

—Sun-Tzu, <u>The Art of War</u>

The old Boy Scout motto, "Be prepared" brings us back to the 5P philosophy: *Prior planning prevents poor performance.* Planning ahead and familiarizing yourself with a new situation will go a long way toward making you look professional. These preparatory steps usually go unnoticed, but they are sure to be noticed if you neglect them!

Parking

Do you know where you will park when you arrive? Will you need to pay a parking meter or attendant? Will your host pick up the tab if you present a receipt? How long will it take you to get to the parking area? Will the time of day (traffic load) make a difference? How long will it take you to get from the parking lot to the room where you are presenting?

I spent many years in Houston, and there were a few things I could always count on: parking was never free; it would take twice as long as expected to drive anywhere; forget trying to get anywhere during rush hour; and expect a long walk from any parking lot or garage. Upon moving to Kansas I had the same initial mentality for several months, and I ended up arriving at appointments 45 minutes early. Eventually I settled into the culture of Kansas and got used to driving across town in 10 minutes, free parking, and easy access.

The point of these stories is that every place is different. The culture of one company may allow you to park next to the building; while another may have you park on the 10th floor of a parking garage. If you are expected to pay for parking and you show up without any money, how will you handle it? Be sure to ask these questions beforehand. Drive the route a day before the presentation and get a feel for it. Is there any construction you did not know about? If you arrive late to a presentation, you will be wasting the time of everyone in the audience. I don't know very many people who enjoy having their time wasted. Out of respect for your audience, do a little preplanning so that you arrive early.

Arrive Early

Why should I arrive early? Won't that just waste my time? A resounding "NO!" is the answer to that question. Arriving early insures that you will be able to start your talk on time and enables you to familiarize yourself with your surroundings and equipment, use the bathroom, and accomplish anything else you may need to do just prior to your talk. The following sections will discuss several of these elements and will explain why you should familiarize yourself with them. In this case, a little bit of knowledge will produce a much more professional and polished presentation.

Meeting Place

Where are you meeting your host? In the auditorium or in an office? Who will be meeting you? Arriving early will provide you enough time to meet the person and have them take you to the presentation room. If you are meeting someone, be sure to tell them you will arrive approximately 30 minutes early and that you would like to familiarize yourself with the room prior to your presentation.

Use the Bathroom

Be sure to use the bathroom within 15 minutes of your presentation. Even if you don't need to, go anyway. That morning cup of coffee may kick in 20 minutes into your 60-

minute talk, and you don't want to end up fidgeting like a little kid or needing to excuse yourself temporarily. Nervousness can, among other things, make you suddenly aware of a need to urinate, even though you didn't have to 5 minutes before. Just "go" and dismiss that worry.

Room

Familiarize yourself with the room you will be speaking in. Does it hold 300 people or 10 people? Will the audience be 3 feet away from you or 30 feet away? Is there a podium? Which side is it on? When you enter the room, stop and take it all in, then walk around the room and get a "feel" for the lighting and acoustics—especially from the back of the room. Then move to the area you will be speaking from and view the room from that position. Take a look at the floor: Are there any cords or holes that you might trip over? Where is the screen located, and how easily can you point to things with a laser pointer? Will you be using a computer mouse instead of a laser pointer? Is there an auxiliary monitor for you to view so that you can always look straight ahead? If you know the answers to these questions, you can walk into the room with confidence when you are introduced.

Lighting

Who will handle the lighting? Are you expected to turn the lights down, or will someone else do this? Does the other person know they are expected to turn the lights down? Do they know how? I once worked at a place that had a spectacularly technologically advanced auditorium. From the podium you could control the entire room. Unfortunately only the people who regularly used the room knew how to control the room; I watched many presenters fumble around with the controls and eventually require help from someone more familiar with the control panel. A few simple questions and instructions prior to your talk will avoid these problems.

Laser Pointer

Using a laser pointer or mouse will help you highlight parts of the presentation. Pointing to objects on screen is not as easy as it sounds; there is an art to properly using a pointer. As with all things, too little is not helpful, and too much is distracting.

To begin with, it is called a *pointer*. Not a circler or an underliner—a *pointer*. Use it to point to things, not to circle them, to underline them, or to wave a red dot violently around the screen. Many people attempt to draw attention to one feature on a slide but fail because they circle a large area instead of pointing to a particular item.

Second, how does the pointer feel in your hands? Is the button easy to push? Does it need new batteries? Don't assume someone else has checked.

Third, your hand is likely to shake a little bit, even if it doesn't in practice. When standing in front of an audience, you will be more nervous than during a practice session. If the screen is far away and your hand shakes even a little bit, the results will be an obvious shake on the screen. Hold the pointer with two hands, or look for a place where you can rest your arm and hand on the podium while pointing to the screen. I once gave a talk to 200 plus people; I arrived early to scope out the room and get my bearings. I knew my hand would shake, so I practiced resting my hand on the podium and was confident I could deal with a little shake. When I rested my hand and turned on the pointer I discovered that the moderator's head was between my resting spot and the computer! I had to find a new spot to rest my hand.

Laser pointers are cheap these days, and, if you will be giving more than a few presentations, I would recommend spending $20 on a decent pointer of your own. A $20 pointer will be sufficient for most rooms. Having one you are familiar with will provide you with just a little more comfort and confidence during your presentation.

As computers in presentations become more and more popular, the laser pointer is being phased out by the computer mouse. While the mouse will help you avoid the shaking commonly seen with a laser pointer, you become tied to the podium. Touchpad mice are not as easy to use as regular mice, and, if you will be using your own laptop, I would suggest bringing a regular mouse that you can attach to your computer. If everything is provided, practice with the mouse to get a feel for it. Some have buttons on the side that may advance the slides if you accidentally push them. It is better to find this out before 100 people are watching you!

Slide Advancer

How will you advance the slides? Directly on the computer? By remote control? By asking a technician to advance them for you? Does the remote need new batteries? Where do you aim it? Here, advanced planning and a few instructions will avoid having to figure it out with a crowd watching you. Fumbling around trying to advance the slides once your presentation has started does not make you look professional.

Some rooms are equipped with a remote control slide advancer. With this, you are not tied to the podium to advance the slides. Most of these remotes are now equipped with a laser pointer also. As always, you need to familiarize yourself with the equipment. One remote I commonly used had the laser pointer button right next to the button that made the screen go black. A slight shift of the finger and I was no longer highlighting an important point on my slide, I was trying to get my slide back on the screen. There are some poor designs in remote control slide advancers and by familiarizing yourself with the equipment, you won't be wondering what happened to your presentation.

Slides

Once you have found out how to use the slide advancer, take a quick run through your slides to make sure they all show up. Mac-to-PC conversions are notorious for causing problems. Pictures that were not embedded into the presentation may actually still be on the computer in your office. In addition to testing my slides on the computer I will be using for the presentation, I also test my presentation on another computer—one that is not attached to the same network. This helps insure that everything SHOULD work properly prior to arriving at the presentation site.

Turn Off Your Cell Phone!!!

We have all been in a lecture, class, movie, funeral, wedding, somewhere, when someone's cell phone starts ringing. You don't want to be that guy during your own talk—I have seen it many times. A good friend forgot to turn off her cell phone during her final presentation of graduate school—someone called her in the middle of her talk.

I also watched someone answer his phone during a speech! However, he needed to take the call, and he explained to us that his entire family had just flown into town and he was meeting them to attend a funeral. We were all willing to give him a few minutes for his call. The point is, if you have an emergency and need to take a call during a presentation, tell the audience why, and they are likely to be forgiving. If you don't tell them, they will assume you are a self-centered jerk!

Water

You will undoubtedly become thirsty during the course of your presentation. Bring your own water bottle; don't rely on someone else to supply you with one! I recommend a bottle because you can screw the cap back on and not worry about spilling it as you reach for it or if you bump the podium.

The Painfully Obvious that Needs No Explanation

- Don't chew gum.
- Dress professionally.
- Speak loudly.
- Speak slowly and enunciate.

Exercises

1. Find a conference room, any conference room, and familiarize yourself with it as described above.

2. Get your hands on a laser pointer and try your hand at pointing to things. Avoid the dreaded laser circle.

Section IV

Giving Your Presentation

With confidence, knowledge, passion for your subject, and a few skills, giving presentations can be a highly enjoyable and rewarding endeavor.

Chapter 9

Engage Your Audience

These investigations revealed that even in such technical lines as engineering, about 15% of one's financial success is due to one's technical knowledge and about 85% is due to skill in human engineering—to personality and the ability to lead people.

—Dale Carnegie, <u>How to Win Friends and Influence People</u>

What does it mean to engage your audience? How can you keep their attention, interact with them during your presentation, and be a vibrant speaker? Engaging your audience involves all of these things and so much more. The basic idea is to grab your audience's attention and keep them captivated for the length of your presentation. Think back to the speakers you have heard that have captivated you for an hour! What did they do that kept your attention? They had great, relevant content; they interacted with the audience, and they identified with you. They may or may not have been dynamic, highly energetic speakers (yes, that helps, but it isn't necessary). They definitely did *not* speak in a monotone fashion or fumble over their words. Their speech was not read word for word or memorized. They had good notes and improvised on the spot as needed.

You do not have to be the most energetic or dynamic person to give a great presentation. Well-prepared content and notes, intimately knowing your presentation aids, passion for your subject, and good audience interaction will allow you to keep the attention of audiences!

Here I will present several ideas for engaging your audience. These are by no means the only ways to engage your audience. As you get more comfortable engaging your audience, study the presenters who do it well. Read more about the topic, and try new things. Some things that work for others may not work for you. Experiment with one or two things at a time and incorporate what works into your style.

Passion for Your Subject Matter

Passion has been defined as "a strong or extravagant fondness, enthusiasm, or desire for anything." If you have a strong passion for your subject matter, it will show through in your presentation. However, even if you don't, you still need to care about your presentation and your audience.

Passion and caring will go a long way toward giving a great talk. In fact, most of the rules you have heard about giving talks are pointless unless you care about your subject matter. The worst talks I have given have been the ones I really didn't care about. And conversely, the best talks I have given have been the ones I deeply cared about and which subject matter I had great passion for. It doesn't matter whether you are talking to your kids or to brilliant scientists, passion, or lack thereof, will come through in your presentation.

Many books and public speaking rules suggest the use of humor to engage your audience and show excitement for your topic. If you are a naturally humorous person and love to tell the latest joke, then by all means, do so! If you are not naturally inclined to have a joke on the tip of your tongue, however, don't tell a joke during your presentation. Your presentation should reflect your personal style, and it is never a good idea to try to fit a square peg into a round hole. That having been said, one of the greatest speakers I know and have been fortunate to study always has a joke handy. It wasn't always used, but when technical difficulties occurred, and the presentation had to be stalled for a few minutes, he was there with a joke ready to make the audience laugh. It was his personal style, and it worked!

To Memorize or Not to Memorize

This is a tough question. Should you memorize your presentation or "wing it"? Neither is the right answer. Memorizing your talk might sound like a good idea, but the second that your train of thought is disrupted, you will have a hard time getting back on track. If you want to memorize your talk, write it out and bring a copy with you to help you get back on track when you get derailed. However, for shorter talks where you have to choose your words carefully, it is a good idea to write it out word for word. Print it in larger-than-normal type size and with space in between the lines.

When a speaker is "just winging it," they can't be derailed. But rare are the people who can "wing" any presentation. Usually these people have given a very similar presentation many times before, so they aren't really "winging it." I have discovered that when I give a presentation, I need to practice it three times. The first time is terrible and lots of changes are made. The second time is ok and gets small changes. The third time is pretty good and only gets tweaked. The fourth time, the actual presentation, is usually great. With little or no preparation, you will easily get lost and fumble for your words and the points you wanted to make.

Well-thought-out notes comprise the best method. For more detailed notes, you can write out all of the points you want to make for each slide and have them on note cards or paper. Another method is to use your slides as your notes. Put just enough information on each one to remind you of what you want to say. This is a very effective method and requires some practice. With your slides as notes, you will be able to move anywhere in the room and have access to your notes. You will appear very professional and knowledgeable about the topic you are presenting.

Get Your Groove On

We have all heard someone tell us they were "in the groove" or "in the zone." *"Everything was going great, and the time flew by."* When you "get into your groove" while you are giving a presentation, the time will fly by, and you will be having fun. When you are in your groove, you don't know it, but when you suddenly notice that you are on your last couple of slides, you have been in the groove. In contrast, the presentations in which I was unable to find my groove seemed to last forever—45 minutes seemed like hours.

What does it take to get in the groove? With a well-prepared talk, good notes, passion for your subject, and confidence, the groove should be easy to find. I have found that it usually takes the first five or ten minutes to get into my groove before things start to flow smoothly. Thus, I plan appropriately, and my first five slides are more simplistic and require less thought to "jog" my memory. Find your groove, and the time will fly by.

Eye Contact

Making eye contact is a great way to identify with your audience. Staring blankly at the back wall or the air above your audience will make you seem nervous, stodgy, and disinterested. Make eye contact with several members of your audience, always shifting and moving around the room, left to right and front to back. Whatever you do, don't stare at one or two people, no matter how good looking they are!

You will quickly go from professional to creepy by staring at one person.

In large auditoriums, you won't actually be able to see individual people, so choose areas. Someone will be there and think you are making eye contact with them. In small groups this will be easy, but pay attention to your target. If you sense that they suddenly seem uncomfortable, move on quickly. If you have friends in the audience, use them! Looking at a friendly face will give you comfort in a roomful of strangers.

Move Around

The eye is naturally drawn to movement against a static background. A little movement will draw attention to you and will help you engage your audience. We have all seen the presenter who is attached to the podium, refusing to leave, and we have seen the other end of the spectrum, with the presenter walking through the audience. The latter is a personal style that most people are not comfortable with, and I would not recommend it for most people, especially beginners. The former is boring—you should not be married to the podium. Instead, use it as an anchor. Move away from the podium, to the side, toward your audience, and back again. As you gain more experience, you will become more comfortable moving around. Take it slow and be patient. It is easy to learn as you gain more experience. If you decide to move to the other side of the room and you have to return to change slides, check your notes, or suddenly point to something, you will appear inexperienced. However, if you move to the other side of the room and return to the podium just in time to switch slides, you will appear experienced and professional. If you find yourself moving around too much or need the confidence of a podium, stand to the side and place one hand on it. In my early presentations I needed the podium not only for emotional support, but also to not be totally exposed to the audience; I would stand beside the podium with one hand on it. Now I occasionally place a hand on the podium to keep myself anchored so I don't wander all over the place. But after 15 years of giving talks and presentations, most of my time is now spent away from the podium.

Name Names

In reference to the previous section about notable people, name names in your presentation. How many times have you called a complete stranger and felt their attitude change immediately upon mentioning a mutual friend? A respected name goes a long way in building instant credibility, however, don't be a name dropper. When it is relevant, don't be afraid to point out the contributions of those who might be in the audience. Everyone will recognize a well-known name, and if they like and respect the person and his or her contributions, you will have gained some credibility and friends just by using it. Using a person's name goes a long way toward creating trust and fellowship; don't be afraid to use it when it is appropriate.

Identify with the Audience

Your audience has come to hear you for a reason. Information—you have it, and they want it. You did not always have this information to share! By telling your audience a little about your background and how you got where you are, you will identify with their current state. Tell them what has helped you and how it can help them. Even though you are the expert in this situation, you do not want to go in and act like an arrogant know-it-all. Before you were an expert, you had to seek information from others also. Approach your presentation from a mentoring standpoint and not a lecturing one.

Telling stories is another great way to identify with your audience and grab their attention. It doesn't have to be your personal story but can be a compelling story that relates to the topic at hand. Think back to the great speakers you have had the opportunity to hear. Their stories were a break from the usual presentation, but they always related to the topic at hand and were able to "drive home" one particular point. Stories have the ability to bring the audience into your presentation on a personal level by tapping into both their mental and emotional sides.

Ask Questions

It is okay to interact directly with your audience. Magicians, clowns, and comedians do this because it is effective. If these skills can keep the attention of a group of five-year-olds, you know it works! Of course, I am not suggesting you pull a coin from the CEO's ear, but you can interact with your audience in a professional and relevant manner. Ask them questions: What is your favorite widget? What is the biggest problem with it? Did you think our last widget was perfect or flawed? Find specific things in your presentation that you can ask your audience's opinion about. Ask questions that you have genuinely had or that you have— even an expert has questions—and this is your chance to pick the brains of 20 people!

Take a quick poll: How many of you have used our widgets before? What is your favorite gadget? In larger audiences, you can ask questions, but don't expect them to answer. Or you can ask rhetorical questions. In smaller audiences, if you really want to, wait for an answer. But if your audience refuses to answer, ask rhetorical questions and don't expect the next question to yield either. Once you have your audience answering questions and talking with you, it will be much easier to interact with them. Direct audience interaction will help to keep them interested (and awake!).

Continual Reinvention

What does it mean to continually reinvent yourself while giving a presentation? Not only do you have to give a presentation, but you have to pay attention to your audience and modify your talk according to their feedback! What do I mean? I mean be responsive to your audience. If you ask questions and all you get are blank stares, stop asking questions. If half of the audience has closed eyes and drooping heads, do something different, loud, and exciting—wake them up! If they look bored or disinterested, or there is a lot of texting going on, try something different because you are not engaging your audience. Of course, you will always have one or two people who are only there for the donuts or because the boss made them attend—they will always be disinterested. Don't try to reinvent yourself for just one or two people, but if half of your audience is bored, try something different.

Eckhart Tolle says in his book, A New Earth, "*The most rigid structures, the most impervious to change, will collapse first.*" He was talking about ideals such as religion and Soviet Communism and not actual structures per se, but his point is applicable to people. You must be willing to change on the fly and reinvent yourself as needed.

Here you will draw upon the small-talk skills you honed earlier in this book. The key to small talk is paying attention to the cues given by the receiver and following up appropriately. This time your receiver happens to be an audience and not a single person. I highly recommend Dale

Carnegie's book, <u>How to Win Friends and Influence People</u>. Study body language, anything about small talk and the king of small talk—flirting. Yes, flirting! Flirting is all about making small talk, and we usually enjoy it more.

Of course, we all know someone who is great at flirting or small talk. Take him or her out and watch how they reinvent themselves on the fly. Study these techniques and styles and translate those same skills to interacting with a group. This takes time to learn, and in your first few presentations you are more likely to be focused on just getting through! When you gain more confidence and become more comfortable in front of audiences, then, and only then, can you begin to learn this valuable skill. Each time you do it, you will feel better, give a better presentation, and notice new cues you have never seen before.

Watch the Clock

Keep an eye on the clock—you don't want to be that guy who won't shut up! If you have built in a premature stopping point— a "Plan B" in case you are running out of time— you will be okay as long as you keep an eye on the clock. When you arrive, find the clock, and make sure you can see it from the podium. If not, use your watch, timer, cell phone, computer, or a friend in the audience. If you find yourself running late, you will have to make a decision about using your early stopping point. Don't be afraid to use it!

When creating a talk, a good rule of thumb is approximately one slide per minute when the presentation is data intensive and requires lots of visual aids. Presentations that do not require many visual aids should have fewer slides, such as one every 2-3 minutes or less. Any more and you will have to talk fast or exceed the given time. Any less and you will end early. When you stand in front of an audience, it is common to speak faster than normal. Thus, if your talk is 65 minutes in a practice session, it will probably be 60 minutes in front of an audience. Don't be alarmed! It is better to end a few minutes early than a few minutes late. However, if you are ahead of schedule, you can slow down and ask your audience a few questions to use up some time. If you are watching the clock appropriately, you can speed up or slow down depending on where you are in your presentation. Only with experience will you learn how to do this.

Exercises

Make a list of five questions you could ask your audience that relate to your talk.

Challenge

Go to a talk, seminar, lecture and pay attention to the audience. What cues are they giving about their interest level and why?

Chapter 10

Driven to Distraction

Are we there yet? How much longer? I spilled my water. He's touching me!

—Every kid in the world

Aaaahhhhhhh! All those stupid noises people make during seminars, classes, and movies! Why can't they realize that other people don't want to hear their cell phones or candy wrappers! Oops, sorry, I was venting a bit, but you know what I am talking about. Perhaps it has been *your* cell phone or pop can? In fact, the last movie I went to, it was *MY* cell phone! I was sure I had turned it off, but I was wrong. Below are a number of distractions you are sure to encounter. There really isn't anything you can do about the distractions except keep your cool, maintain a positive attitude, and keep on going.

Cell Phones

Cell phones are perhaps the single greatest distraction and annoyance during any presentation. As cell phones grow in usage, they only increase in annoyance. Have you been to a movie lately? I am old enough to remember the days when cell phones didn't exist, and if you wanted to make a call you went to the lobby and dropped a dime (yes, a dime) into the payphone. Today you will see a preview notice reminding (or highly encouraging) you to turn off your phone. Despite the "please turn off your phone" message, some people will ignore it and their phones will ring. They will text; some will even answer the phone and talk! I have given lots of talks to a room full of physicians who were on-call so pagers and cell phones often went off. Because I knew this about my audience, these interruptions did not surprise me and I was not distracted by the cell phones and pagers.

It is perfectly fine if you want to courteously remind others to turn their phones and pagers to vibrate or silent mode before your presentation, but don't expect it to happen. And when one rings you do not need to point out the offending person. It will be pretty obvious who it is, and they will be fully embarrassed. Just keep talking.

The Guy Next to You

If you are in a small room, you may have to deal with people right next to you. They may fidget, move around, and even extend their legs into your walking space. While you can't do anything about fidgety people (I am one of them), if someone moves into your space, you can ask him or her politely to move back a bit:

"Please move your legs out of my aisle."

If the person is even minimally observant and you can catch his or her eye, simply pointing to the offending body part might do the trick. This is a safety issue. You don't want to trip while moving around the room.

You will almost always find those two people who want to have a private conversation during your presentation. You have to learn to ignore these offending people. However, if you find yourself having to talk over them, kindly ask them to stop their discussion or take it outside. Also remember to read your audience: Are the talkers disturbing others in your audience? If so, kindly ask them to refrain from their conversation. Remember, you're in charge.

Food

Many presentations are accompanied by catered food. If not, someone is likely to bring something in. Usually food per se, isn't much of a problem, but opening a pop can or bottle can easily be a distraction. Rest assured that the distraction from a pop can will quickly be over. It will be loud and short. Lunch presentations can be a lot of fun. However, if lunch is being served, it's a guarantee that people will be eating, moving around, and making noise. While this may sound tricky, lunch presentations are usually less formal, and interaction with your audience will be easier.

Spills

On rare occasions, you will have a giant distraction of someone spilling his or her coffee or water. Just make sure it isn't you—use a bottle instead of a cup for your water. You will not need to clean the spill, but you will need to evaluate the situation and decide whether to take a short break or to keep going. Usually someone hosting will take charge of the situation; follow his or her lead.

Technical Difficulties

If you give very many presentations, you will eventually have some kind of technical difficulty. These can include a number of things: microphones, computer, slides, projectors, lights; anything you can think of can and will go wrong—remember Murphy's Law! But if you have prepared properly and have shown up early, these technical difficulties will often be beyond your control and will be reduced in frequency. The key for you is *not* to fix these problems, but instead to know how to assess and handle the situation. If the microphone goes out in a small room, just talk louder; if it goes out in an auditorium with 800 people, you will need to stop until it works again.

The most common problem I have seen is slides that do not show up on the computer. This can be caused by numerous reasons. If you have provided the equipment, you will need to fix it while continuing your talk. If the equipment is provided for you, a technician should be available to fix it. If you know your slides well or keep a print out or outline handy, you can simply describe what is on them.

If technical difficulties cause a delay at the beginning of your talk, you can introduce yourself and start your talk (or tell a joke). When the slides come back up you can then quickly skip through the first few introductory slides. When things go wrong, you don't want to be a deer in the headlights. The ability to properly deal with technical difficulties displays a high level of professionalism.

Challenge

1. Don't be "that guy." Identify the ways you are a distraction.

2. Think through a "Plan B" in case everything technical that can go wrong does!

Chapter 11
Silence Is Golden

Express yourself completely,

then keep quiet. Be like the forces of nature:

when it blows, there is only wind;

when it rains, there is only rain;

when the clouds pass, the sun shines through.

—Lao-Tzu, <u>Tao Te Ching</u>

We all have those annoying little things that we do and say to fill the void of silence. *Yes, even you.* I have taken it upon myself to launch a one-man campaign to rid the English language of that dreadful word, "*Uh.*" Most of us don't realize how many times we say *"uh," "ah,"* or some version of it until we have viewed a video of ourselves or a kind honest soul points it out to us.

Early in my career I told my advisor that he said *"uh"* a lot and asked if he realized it. He vehemently denied it and *"uh"* said he *"uh"* never says it. (See, "uh" is hard to read, so why is it so easy to say?) I was a wise young student and had counted the number of times he said the word *"uh."* When I told him he said it 27 times in one minute, he was shocked! He quickly mended his ways and erased the word from his vocabulary. Most of us do these things but just don't realize it. Record yourself and get the honest truth.

Filling the Void

These types of words are used to fill silence or when we are momentarily thinking; and all we can utter is a poor attempt at a word. Filling the void is not necessary. In fact, these moments of silence are so brief that if they actually existed no one would even notice them. People would think you are just taking a breath. If the void is long enough to notice, they are likely to think that you have paused for dramatic effect— let them think that.

Verbalizing a thinking *"uh"* is painfully obvious and reveals that you don't really know what to say at that very moment. Here again, silence is golden. A silent pause won't even be noticed, but an extended utterance of *"uhhhhh"* will be. A presentation filled with 500 pauses no longer than a breath will be a great presentation, but a presentation filled with 500 *"uhs"* will be noticed and talked about in your absence.

Five hundred! Are you kidding? I would never say "uh" 500 times. I commonly run into people who say *"uh"* more than 10 times each minute of speaking! A low number is three times, but three is still too many. Remember the guy who said it 27 times in one minute? Three per minute for a 60-minute talk would be 180 times! And 27 times per minute would be 1620 *"uhs"* in 60 minutes! You don't want to be known as the *"uh"* guy—strike this word and all its cousins from your vocabulary.

Practice! Practice! Practice!

The key to overcoming these dreaded words is practice and lots of it. Pay attention to yourself when you talk: How often do you have a void-filling word inserted into a conversation? It probably happens more often than you think. When you first begin trying to eliminate these dreaded utterances, you will stumble around as you begin to notice yourself saying these words. After a few practice sessions, you will be at ease allowing silence to fill the voids.

As you go to seminars and presentations, count the number of times other speakers use these words. After reading this chapter you will notice them more and more, and you should become sufficiently annoyed by them. I am always looking for more people to help me rid the world of these pseudo attempts at words.

Exercises

1. Record yourself. Sound only will work well enough. Identify your void-filling word or words. Count the number of times you say that word in one minute.

2. Practice what you just recorded yourself doing and try to eliminate your "special" words.

Challenge

Have a friend help you with the exercises.

Section V

The Dreaded Inquisition!

Have patience and answer only the questions asked.

Chapter 12

How to Handle Questions and Answers

You can't handle the truth!

—Col. Jessop, *A Few Good Men*

This line from the movie, *A Few Good Men,* demonstrates how questions and answers can be a frightening prospect. Questions can be the most frightening part of your presentation because you are suddenly in the hot seat and only have a few seconds to prepare. But since you are an expert on this topic, you should do well with a few pointers and a little practice. In fact, if you are well prepared, the interactions during Q&A sessions can turn out to be the most enjoyable part of your presentation.

Have Patience

Often I have tried to ask a question, but the speaker began answering before I finished the question. These cases usually involve arrogant people who presume to know what I am asking. If they would simply wait for me to finish my sentence, they would understand the question and be able to provide me with the information I am seeking, not information *they* think I am seeking. Have patience and let your audience member finish the question—don't interrupt. It is rude; it makes them upset, and it makes you look arrogant.

After the participant has finished the question, don't start talking immediately. Take a second or two to think about the question and your answer. This brief pause will allow you to formulate a great answer that is appropriate to the question instead of rambling through some unnecessary information and giving a long-winded, incoherent response. I have counseled many beginning speakers, and this is probably the number-one bad habit that has to be broken. In addition, people who start answering immediately tend to talk faster and ramble longer. Taking a second or two to collect your thoughts will slow down your pace, and you will appear to be more reflective, intelligent, and professional. In the beginning, count to three after a question—this short pause won't even be noticed.

Think About the Question

Now that you have learned to take a few seconds to formulate an answer, you have to start by thinking about the question. What was asked? Will a yes or no answer be sufficient, or does it require an explanation? Here the "KISS" philosophy comes in handy: *Keep it simple stupid!* Don't overcomplicate the question. Most often the simplest and shortest answer is the best. Also think about the context of your presentation. If you are an engineer and speaking to accountants, you have worked hard to make your presentation in accountant lingo, don't suddenly fall back into engineering language.

Can You Please Rephrase Your Question?

It is not uncommon to receive a question you just don't understand. The worst thing you can do is try to answer something you don't understand—you will only sound like a lost fool. If you don't understand the question, ask the person to rephrase it. Reply with a simple, *"I am sorry. I am not quite sure what you are asking. Can you please rephrase your question?"*

Most people will be happy to do this. You can also repeat the question in your own words. This will give you a few more moments to process a response and show the person asking the question whether you understand the question—or not.

Experienced and confident presenters are not afraid to use these techniques when necessary. However, don't overuse them in the same presentation. It is better to sound a little confused over a question than to ramble on about butterflies when the person wanted to know about grasshoppers. Your audience will know you didn't understand the question, and it will be discussed in your absence.

Repeat the Question

I have mild hearing loss, so I often have to ask people to repeat their question a little louder—sometimes a lot louder.

"I couldn't hear you. Can you please repeat that a little louder?"

Many factors can cause you to be unable to hear the question. For me, mild hearing loss makes it difficult to hear high-pitched voices and strong accents. Many people have quiet voices and are often asked to speak up. It is a treat when someone asks a question and his or her voice booms above everything else, allowing you and the audience to hear everything clearly. Other factors such as outside noise or room distractions can also cause difficulty in hearing questions. Referring back to the *Driven to Distraction* section, you may also find these same distractions recurring, making it difficult for you to hear the question. When (notice I said when, not if) this happens, it will usually be obvious to everyone involved, and the inquirer is happy to repeat the question, just louder this time.

It is also a good idea to repeat or rephrase all of the questions you are asked. This will clarify the question for both you and the audience. In larger settings, your entire audience is unlikely to have heard the question. They will hear your answer, but they won't know the context. In very large settings, the person asking the question will probably be asking from a microphone, so repeating the question isn't necessary. In small settings, the room is probably small enough that everyone can hear the question, too.

Repeating the question insures that your entire audience heard the question and will understand your answer. When you see presenters using this technique, they always appear to be extremely experienced, and their presentations end with an air of experience-induced confidence.

Stop Talking and Just Answer the Question!

When we get nervous or don't know the answer, we tend to just start talking. I have worked with many people who opened his or her mouth and just started talking as soon as possible after the question was finished. Nervousness and inexperience lead some people to spew all of the information they know about a topic, hoping the answer will be in there somewhere.

Don't vomit information! Politicians are good at this; they can speak for ten minutes and say nothing of value. You are still left wondering what the answer is, and by now you have forgotten the question and are focusing on the ability of this person to waste five minutes with *blah, blah, blah.* If you are patient and understand the question, you will be able to formulate a good answer. Focus on giving an answer that answers just the question and nothing more. This is a skill that can only be learned through practice.

Sincerity

This may sound like a strange topic to insert into a Q&A discussion, but the importance of being sincere cannot be overstated. You are probably giving a presentation to people with whom you are currently doing or want to do business. If you are not sincere and truthful in your words and actions, you will lose much more than the sale.

Just before our second child was born, we were searching for a newer, bigger vehicle. A used-car salesman called to say he had the perfect car for us and I had better hurry in because it wouldn't last long. I was young and naïve, so I rushed over to test drive the car.

The salesman kept telling me about the side-view mirror, "It folds in."

"Great," I said, "but what size is the engine?"

"I don't know," replied the salesman, "but the mirror folds in."

This salesman was not sincere when he called and told me he had the perfect car for me. Not only did he lose that particular sale, but the dealership lost my business. If they were going to employ people who didn't care about my needs, I didn't want to do business with them!

If any man thinks he can build up a successful career on pretences and appearances, let him pause before sinking into the abyss of shadows; for the insincerity there is no solid ground, no substance, no reality; there is nothing on which anything can stand and no material with which to build; but there are loneliness, poverty, shame, confusion, fears, suspicions, weeping, groaning, and lamentations; for if there is one hell lower, darker, fouler than all others, it is the hell of insincerity.

—James Allen, <u>As a Man Thinketh</u>

Be truthful and honest throughout your presentation, and it will come through in your answers to the questions presented. A lack of sincerity will also come through, and the audience will either destroy you or ignore you—either way you have lost the sale.

I Don't Know

How many times have we been asked a question and we didn't know the answer? How many times today? In a one-on-one setting we are not afraid to say, "I don't know." It isn't threatening to our pride and ego to say "I don't know" to our friends. Our friends know we don't have all the answers, and we don't pretend we do. So why do we have a problem saying "I don't know" in front of a crowd?

Audience members are just individual people who know we are not encyclopedias. It is better to admit you don't know than to give incorrect information.

"I don't know" is an acceptable answer—use it wisely.

You Can't Win an Argument

Occasionally you will have an audience member who wants to argue with you. This can be a complete stranger or the antagonistic person described previously. You CAN'T win an argument, so don't even try! You are on their turf, and we all know about the home-field advantage. This person is usually obstinate and wants to be right at all costs. Take the "high road," the professional road, and don't let yourself be lured into an argument. You are on stage, and you need to maintain control of the situation. Use responses like these:

"Thank you for your comment."

"That is an interesting viewpoint."

"I will take that into consideration."

"Thank you, but let's move on."

Such statements will quickly diffuse the situation and establish you as the leader. If a question is asked, you can give a brief, nonconfrontational answer followed by, *"Let's move on. Next question please."*

Only the most vocal or obstreperous people will continue after this exchange. Take the "high road" and be professional.

Is There a Question Somewhere in There?

Some questions are really comments—take them as such. If it is obvious the person is making a comment, thank them for their input and move on to the next question. If you are not sure, you can ask, *"Is there a question in there?"* Or you can simply reply with a comment of your own.

Sometimes these comments can be extremely helpful and provide a new insight into the issue at hand. Sometimes the person simply wants to point out his or her or a friend's contributions to the widget industry. This is okay—don't let it rattle or distract you. Simply thank them, briefly comment, and move on.

Seek Out Advice

Seeking the advice of friends and colleagues about the audience before your presentation can give you great insight into the individuals you will face. You will know whose name to mention in your talk. If you have a prominent person in your audience and you mention his or her name and how you agree with his or her work and philosophies, they are less likely to argue with you during the Q&A. After all, if you agree with him or her, then he or she would basically be arguing with himself or herself.

You can also find out whom to avoid calling on. The best feeling is when you have predicted what questions the argumentative person will ask. With good planning and experience, this becomes easy. When a certain audience member asks you about the new notch in the widget, you can have a prepared slide ready to show them with a lead in, such as *"I thought you might ask that."*

Knowledge of your audience is important, but you must also act on this knowledge. Usually friends and colleagues are thrilled when you ask their advice—we all like to be asked for advice.

Anecdotal Stories

Here are some stories to demonstrate how most people inherently have the ability to answer questions in a way that is appropriate for any audience. When problems occur, they are usually easily identified and remedied by honest evaluation of your skills. The exercises at the end of this chapter can help you work toward this goal.

I was once given the charge to help a young man develop the skills to answer questions appropriately. Before I met with him, all I knew was that he had failed miserably and I could help him. I didn't know what the problem was going in, but within 10 seconds of his first answer it was obvious—too much detail. In fact, the amount of detail he spewed verged on the absurd. A one-sentence answer somehow developed into an entire commentary— and that was just the introduction to the answer. With a little practice and coaching, he learned to answer questions in an appropriate and succinct manner.

Another man gave short answers; he inaccurately assumed we knew the background information and therefore gave us the shortest answer possible. Because of this, he appeared arrogant. With a little help, he learned to give the appropriate amount of background information for his audience.

One of the more challenging people I have worked with had the confidence to answer, but did not have the knowledge to formulate an appropriate answer. After several sessions of working with this particular woman, she learned to draw upon the facts she had to first think about the question and then develop an answer that could be supported by her current knowledge. The answer didn't have to be 100% correct, just supported by facts. Practice was an important part of her development.

Sometimes people can give great answers and are just fine without any help. I have worked with lots of people who didn't need any help at all, but by practicing they were able to hone their skills and increase their abilities—and their comfort levels.

Exercises

1. Find a small group of people (less than three). Ask each other questions and give answers.

2. Evaluate the answers and provide honest feedback. If someone in your group does not give honest feedback, replace them.

Challenge

In your small group, discuss and predict the questions your coworkers may ask. The better you know them, the more accurate your predications will be.

Chapter 13
Q&A Styles

What we have here is a failure to communicate.

—The Captain, *Cool Hand Luke*

I particularly like this quote from the movie *Cool Hand Luke* because it represents the inability of two people to see eye-to-eye in a situation. Luke refuses to "get with the program" in the prison system, and the Captain refuses to understand that Luke will not be broken. Two people are unable to understand each other and unwavering in their stance. Q&A sessions can be lots of fun if you approach them from an open-minded, mentoring stance. Having a close-minded attitude, not listening to the questions, or providing inappropriate answers will only lead to a failure to communicate.

There are basically four types of Q&A styles you will encounter during live presentations. Since you are giving the presentation, you can help guide the audience and use the style that works best for you.

One-on-One

This is the most informal style of Q&A and is usually the most comfortable. One-on-one is more like a conversation than an official presentation. However, you will need to have your elevator speech handy to give them information. After all, they came to see you and to get information, not to hear you ramble aimlessly. With a conversation, you can give answers specifically geared towards the person asking the questions— if he or she wants more detail he or she can ask. You can also ask him or her questions.

You are also free to ask their opinions and to ask them questions. Who knows? You may have just found your next collaborator or business partner. Poster presentations and tradeshow booths use this style. Information gathering occurs in a personal manner. The give and take of information will flow both ways and can be mutually beneficial. Here you will interact more intimately and with fewer people compared with the other styles.

Small Group

Small groups can range from 3 to 20 people, and the dynamics of the small group will change as the group becomes larger. Smaller groups will compare more closely to one-on-one interactions, and bigger groups will gravitate toward large group dynamics.

The smaller the group, the more likely they are to interact with you. For instance, in small groups you may be asked to explain something, answer a question, or field a comment during your presentation. In larger groups, this normally won't happen. The smaller group appears less formal than a larger group and thus opens the door to more informal questioning styles. Here you will want to provide enough detail to answer the question in a succinct manner. If they want more detail, they will probably come see you afterward. However, most of the audience probably does not want to know the answer in the greatest detail possible.

At the beginning of your talk, you have the option of asking the audience to hold questions until the end or allowing them to intervene anytime. In small groups, I prefer the latter because it makes the presentation less formal and allows you to more effectively engage your audience.

Workshop

Workshop settings operate like a small group only with constant interruptions. The purpose of a workshop is to acquire and practice the information being presented. You are likely to be bombarded with questions constantly, and you will probably need to use a whiteboard (chalkboard for the older folks and SMART Board for the younger) as an aid in answering questions. (See the next chapter for a discussion on Q&A with whiteboards.) The ebb and flow of information and interaction with the audience can be a fun experience for all.

Large Group

Large group settings are the most formal type you will encounter. They can range from 20 people to thousands. Again, the smaller the group, the greater the level of interaction, and the larger the group, the less interaction there will be. Groups or around 20 people may ask some questions during your presentation, but groups over 100 will definitely hold their questions and comments until the end. For these larger groups, you will need to repeat the question and give short, simple, general answers—don't go into great detail.

Exercises

1. As you are practicing answering questions with the small group you established in the last chapter, try giving answers targeted toward both a small group and a large group.
2. Try answering the same question with multiple follow-up questions to give greater detail. This will simulate one-on-one situations.

Chapter 14

The *Art* of the Board

First comes thought; then organization of that thought into ideas and plans; then transformation of those plans into reality. The beginning, as you will observe, is in your imagination.

—Napoleon Hill

Standing in front of a group of people and answering questions is one thing, but writing your answers on a large board while talking to an audience requires a whole different set of skills. Those who do it well make it look like an art form. Think back to your college professors; who used a board well and who did not? The ones who did were able to get the information across considerably more effectively than those who did not. This is an art form more than a skill because it requires you to put together many of the skills you have learned already into one beautiful auxiliary communication method. However, one person may think your board work is genius, while the person sitting next to him or her may wonder what you are trying to do.

Planning Your Answer

Writing on a board allows you to convey much more information and to give more detailed answers than is possible by only talking. Here it is very important to have some patience and to plan your answer. What will you write? Will a graph or a diagram make the point more clear? Can I draw a picture? With a board and marker you can do anything your creativity will allow—just don't overdo it.

The Beginning

Always start on the left-hand side of the board, no matter what— that is, your audience's left, not the direction you happen to be facing. Our eyes naturally go from left to right (with some exceptions), Even if you think you have a short answer and will only need a small section of the board, start on the left side. This enables you to expand your answer and to add more details and diagrams if you feel they are needed.

I have often started to draw a picture and then realized that my stick bunny was not turning out to be the size I thought it should be. The result was a giant stick bunny next to a scrunched up stick person, and no where left for me to write anything else! By starting on the far left you will ensure that you have board space left to enlarge your answer.

A second reason for starting on the far left is that you may not have to erase your drawings in order to answer the next question. And if you can save your erasing for later, do so.

(Your audience did not come to watch you erase the board.) You may also discover the next question is a follow-up question or builds on the graph you just drew. If you have erased the graph, you will have to spend precious time drawing it again. After hearing the next question and planning your answer, you can decide whether to build on your previous answer or erase it and start over. Start on the far left side of the board, and don't erase an answer until you need the space.

Be Succinct

We have developed the elevator speech, and we have learned how important it is to be succinct. Now it is time to apply these ideas to Q&A. Not every word needs to be written— just the important ones. Practice will help you get the important words on the board without sacrificing meaning.

If your handwriting is lousy, avoid writing words or take extra care to make sure they are legible. My handwriting is atrocious, so I draw diagrams and graphs and spend extra time making sure the words are legible. When writing words, make them large, even if they seem gigantic to you. You are

12 inches from the board, but your audience is 10 feet (and often more) away. They need to be able to see them.

A Picture Says a Thousand Words

Should I draw a picture? Yes, absolutely! Pictures and diagrams can make your points more understandable than simply using words to describe them. With a little practice you will be able to draw a simple picture more quickly than you could describe it. Practice drawing simple pictures of things that are important to your industry.

If you will be drawing graphs, don't forget to label the axes. If you do forget, your answer will lack important information. Observe the example on the next page. In the upper graph, you have no idea what the graph means; however, when six words are added in the lower graph, the meaning of the graph becomes very clear. Don't leave your audience confused or guessing what your graph is all about.

Drawing pictures and graphs on paper with a sharp pencil is one thing, but drawing them on a large board with a fat marker while standing and talking is a much more difficult task!

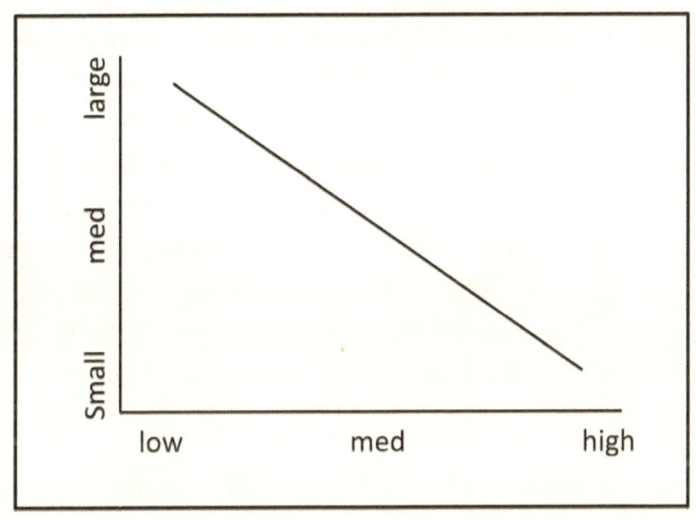

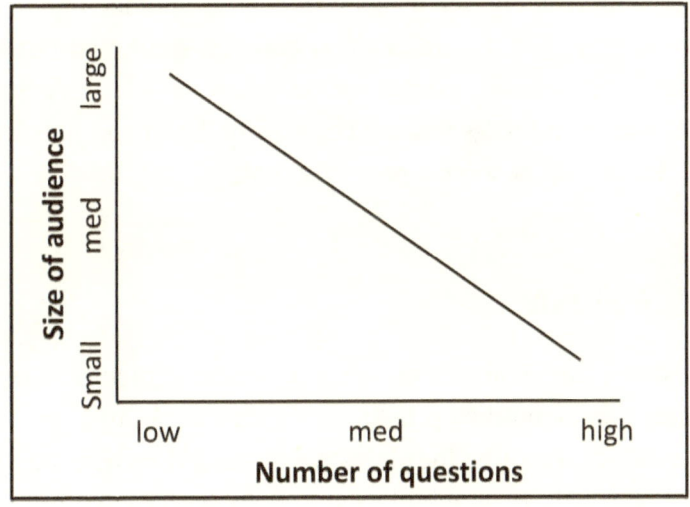

Just Because You Can Doesn't Mean You Should

Many whiteboards and conference rooms come pre-stocked with five different colors of pens. *Before you use any marker on a whiteboard, MAKE SURE IT IS A DRY-ERASE MARKER.* It will say "dry-erase" or will have the brand name of the board company on it. If you are in doubt, don't use it, or ask someone. *If it says "Sharpie," don't use it!* Arriving early has many advantages; ascertaining the conditions and materials for board use are certainly among them! In fact, if I know I will be using a whiteboard, I will bring my own markers.

You may be tempted to use all the colors available to make a beautifully colorful picture. *Don't!* Choose a dark color as your base, preferably black. If it doesn't write and is dried out, immediately set it aside and grab another one—don't panic, it is just a marker. You can use additional colors to highlight specific points or to show a clear difference between two things you are comparing. Use them judiciously and they will become a powerful tool.

Keep on Talkin'

Just because you are drawing a beautiful picture does not mean you should stop talking. You are creating a visual aid on the fly. Just like the slides we discussed earlier, the visual aid is exactly that, an aid used to help describe a point. Your words should add more information and describe the visual aid you are presenting. A few seconds of silence is golden, but do not create 30 seconds of silence while you draw a stick bunny and his family.

Don't Turn Your Back on Me!

You may be tempted to face the board as you are writing. Try not to turn your back toward your audience for very long. With practice, you can learn to write sideways. Also keep turning your head toward your audience as you continue speaking. This will help to keep your audience engaged, and you can use their reactions to your drawings to adjust them as needed.

Exercises

1. Time yourself: How long does it takes to <u>write</u> your elevator speech? It may be succinct for speaking but not for writing.

2. How can you succinctly write your elevator speech?

3. Draw a picture and describe it in words. What details can be removed without losing the purpose of the picture?

Challenge

1. Grab your small group friends and practice answering questions using a board.

2. Develop some common drawings you may need to make, such as graphs, people, or widgets. Practice drawing them while standing at a board and talking.

Conclusions

Mastering the skills of Live Presentations was developed from more than fifteen years of experience giving live presentations and counseling countless people in various situations. Each person has strengths and weaknesses. I hope this work will enable you to identify yours so you can harness your strengths and target your weaknesses. This book is not meant to provide all the answers or to be your only source. However, it will give you a solid foundation to build upon as you learn and gain more speaking experience.

With some confidence and a few skills, live presentations can be fun and rewarding. With practice and preparatory effort, standing up in front of 100 people who came to hear you speak can become a worthwhile endeavor. Enjoy the tremendous adrenaline rush that comes from knowing all your preparations have paid off and that you did a great job!

References and Further Reading

1. James Allen, <u>As a Man Thinketh</u>, 1903
2. Dale Carnegie, <u>How to Win Friends and Influence People,</u> Revised Edition, 1936
3. T.S. Eliot, <u>Knowledge and Experience in the Philosophy of F.H. Bradley</u>, 1964
4. Debra Fine, <u>The Fine Art of Small Talk</u>, 2005
5. Napoleon Hill, <u>Think and Grow Rich</u>, 1937
6. Robert T. Kiyosaki, with Sharon L. Lechter, <u>Rich Dad Poor Dad</u>, 1997
7. Tyler H. McCormick, Matthew J. Salganik, Tian Zheng, "How many people do you know?: Efficiently estimating personal network size." Department of Statistics, Columbia University, New York, September 17, 2008
8. Dan Miller, <u>48 Days to the Work You Love</u>, 2005
9. Eckhart Tolle, <u>A New Earth, Awakening to Your Life's Purpose</u>, 2008
10. Sun-Tzu, <u>The Art of War</u>, Translated by Lionel Giles, 2010
11. Choose the Right Colors for Your PowerPoint Presentation, Accessed October 12th, 2010
    http://office.microsoft.com/en-us/PowerPoint-help

About the Author

Matthew Herynk is currently owner and president of ProAbstract, LLC, a life science and healthcare communications consulting company. He began his public speaking career in high school with church readings and debate competitions. His college and graduate school experiences brought him in contact with skillful mentors who taught him how to present data-intensive content to a diverse array of audiences. In graduate school at the University of Texas-Houston Health Science Center, he quickly gained a reputation as the "go-to guy" for an honest opinion and personalized coaching. Throughout his educational and professional career, he has continued the tradition handed down to him by his advisors and mentored others in the art of successful presentations.

Matthew H. Herynk, Ph.D
matt.herynk@proabstractllc.com
www.proabstractllc.com

Index

www.ingramcontent.com/pod-product-compliance
Lightning Source LLC
Chambersburg PA
CBHW022000170526
45157CB00003B/1078